A trilogy
by Yannis Andricopoulos

In Bed with Madness

The Greek Inheritance

The Future of the Past

To Paddy

Published in the UK by Imprint Academic
PO Box 200, Exeter EX5 5HY, UK

Published in the USA by Imprint Academic
Philosophy Documentation Center
PO Box 7147, Charlottesville, VA 22906-7147, USA

ISBN 978-1845401290

A CIP catalogue record for this book is available from the
British Library and US Library of Congress

www.imprint-academic.com

Yannis Andricopoulos

In Bed with Madness

Trying to Make Sense in a World that Doesn't

Contents

Part I: 'M' for Madness

Back in 1936 Dylan Thomas, the Welsh poet, offered guests at the International Surrealist Exhibition teacups full of boiled string asking them politely if they wanted their drink weak or strong. The media, of course, had a field day – 'a travesty of everything that's decent', the newspapers barked. 'Decent' obviously was what confirms the madness of a civilisation which debases everything, treats it like firewood. Conversely, indecent is the parody of its madness. Many exhibitions later, and while we are still dancing to the tuneless music of our madness, we can look back in awe and reverence at the inexhaustible reserves of our adaptive capability. In spite of everything, global warming, bush fires, nuclear weapons, Aids, drugs, McDonald's, reality-TV and sperm-banks, we are still around, looking forward to the replacement of our hormones and watching *The Jerry Springer Show*. The frog in the pot that never realised the gradual rise in temperature until it was too late was, I think, as adaptable.

Madness, to which we are as attached as a funeral junkie is to funerals, makes its case on rational grounds. Hence it is not recognised as such. Pedestrian in its looks and unassuming in its claims, inextricably linked to everyday life, indeed, the third party in our *ménage à trois* with life, it is, instead, our normality.

The mechanisms of what we call abnormal behaviour, Sigmund Freud demonstrated, are ever present in what is considered normal life. They are easily traceable in the values and the norms of a society which views anything real as irrational and anything

5

rational as unreal, in our communication with the world in line with the requirements of conformity or the anonymous pressure of the group. They are ever-present in the merciless language of non-madness which commands respectability in the press rooms, boardrooms and our own living rooms, indeed, in our entire culture which has been surreptitiously forced to succumb to the irrational. Unaware of alternatives, we view any attempt to escape from the world of unaccountable madness as an attempt to run into its world. Life is apparently a prison without an outside. Indeed, as Blaise Pascal, the seventeenth century French philosopher, said, 'men are so necessarily mad, that not to be mad would be to give a mad twist to madness'.

The man of madness is in this sense not Jaroslav Hasek's fellow who thought he was the sixteenth volume of Otto's encyclopaedia. It is, instead, the man of 'Reason' at home with the claims of freedom, science, progress, economic growth or civilisation, all of which represent both Reason's triumph and betrayal.

In the Kandinsky painting in which we dwell, nothing much seems to be either mental or psychological disorder. Ignoring the plea of the wretched and disempowered is normal; answering savagery with savagery is rational; bombing alien populations, those who have never heard of the Dow Jones or the benefits of psychoanalysis, is anything but inherently insane. The brutal display of power, the slaughtering of the world's poorest by the world's richest, the despatch during the wars of the twentieth century alone of two hundred and fifty million people to what poet Pablo Neruda so delicately called 'the other shore of the sea which has no other shore' – they are all normal. To bomb, destroy, exterminate, eliminate, pulverise and devastate, to carry on with old routines which at the end will force us to kiss the abyss is as natural as a door banging in the wind. Abnormal, mad, insane is considered, instead, the refusal to kill fellow human beings.

'Normal', too, is living with extreme poverty, violence or environmental degradation, the rationalisation of domination, exploitation and oppression, the global criminal economy or the brutal use of force as the only answer to the problems of the age. The same perverted logic reigns over the entire spectrum of human activity. To protect ourselves, we stockpile nuclear, chemical and biological weapons which can only annihilate life on the planet; to increase our wealth, we ruthlessly exploit the earth that sustains our wellbeing; to support our values, we resort to action which obliterates them. 'All my means are sane,' Captain Ahab, the quintessential American, said in Herman Melville's *Moby-Dick*, 'my ends alone are mad.'

Just as perverted is the opposition to the madness of modernism by the madness of the insane – the Islamic, Christian and Jewish fundamentalists, heirs of Abraham's monotheistic baggage. They unleash the darkest, the gloomiest, the most primitive forces in the human psyche, and threaten to bring the day of the final catastrophe, the doom day, as close as their next prayer to God.

The entire modern civilisation claims to rest on sovereign Reason which is, surely, nothing but sterile madness masquerading as Reason. Its quintessence is in the veins of a system that thrives on inequality both within and between nations, razes old cultures to the ground and has reduced nature, humans and values to mere means, commodities and resources to be exploited. In its realm, things other than 'us' are nothing but objects for our gratification, means for the consummation of our precious love affair with ourselves, entities to be manipulated for all the material benefits they provide. Ostensibly 'value free', white as a lily in May, the free market has no objective other than profit, the sole point of reference before, within and after history, if capitalism is to be believed. Its monoculture, pursued regardless of the crass commodification of all things, the homogenisation of all life on earth and even our denial as human beings has redefined reality itself. It has thrown the totality of our existence, valued not for what it is, but for the monetary value it represents, into a state of crisis.

Justice, which as a concept rests on boundaries, respect for the whole and all its parts, fair distribution of all goods, and self-imposed limits, including limits to power, has in the process been reduced to an ideal of lost content known only by its silences. Its spirit, 'never broken but for gain' to paraphrase John Dryden, has become a flimsy memory of our cravings, the translucent monument to our delusions, another commodity with prime entertainment value. Turned by capitalism into a legalistic, retributive process, it only strengthens the arm of its law enforcers. On the other hand, when degraded by religious fundamentalism to a prurient morality, it repels. Adolf Eichmann, happy to supervise Hitler's 'final solution', while in prison, would not touch Vladimir Nabokov's *Lolita*, such an 'unwholesome' book. His stock of decency is just as pitiful as that of our culture of which he was a product.

This is our normality, normal as necrophiliac masturbation. Its 'universe of monitored pollution, apocalyptic security, programmed education, medicalised sickness, computer-managed death and other forms of institutionalised nonsense is so frightening', Austrian-born philosopher and social historian Ivan Illich said in horror, 'that I can face it with the respect due to the devil.' But, of course, despite all this we are free – free to express our authentic sexual self, safari in the Serengeti, or vote for our favourite TV character while looking forward to more technological advances which one day may give us a paperless office and possibly a paperless toilet too.

It follows that we do not find anything strange in the exploitation of our illusions, the homelessness of our minds, the computerisation of our lives, the commodification of our existence and the dismantlement of our bonds with our family and our community. Nor do we find strange the compartmentalisation and sullen loneliness of a hectic life, the marginalisation of the individual, the powerlessness which has transformed us into pathetic spectators of life as shown on TV, and much more, including the death of a whole species of feelings and of our dreams. In the 'ocean of veiled hostility' in which we sail, 'normal', too, is our alienation from our inner selves, bodies, spirituality, sexuality and sensitivity, the repression of our instinctual drives, the tormenting lack of self-confidence and self-respect or our efforts to mimic naturalness, the burnouts, the obsessions, the addictions, the compulsions, the depression and the eating disorders, the broken emotional bonds, the craving for meaning, purpose and a sense of belonging, and the years we never lived.

This is indeed our 'normality' which Leo Tolstoy's Ivan Ilych had no hesitation to turn into 'the goal at which he aimed in family life.' 'The rat in the Skinner box, mindlessly and monotonously working and consuming in its barren, structured environment', Nick Heather, a clinical psychologist, wrote, 'is a parody of modern man's situation'. Occasionally we may, of course, end up clamouring, like Nietzsche's Zarathustra, 'I want to learn to be human again.' But this seems destined only to take us to Oxford Street, which, thankfully, can take care of our disenchantments as it was, perhaps, decreed by the original intention.

Our minds can trudge unconcernedly through the ruins of our relationship with our cities, the environment, the planet, politics, science or education, past, present and future. They watch with radiant indifference at what the Frankfurt School philosopher Jürgen Habermas calls the crisis of rationality, of legitimacy, and of motivation. They accept unquestioningly, as the leading ecosocialist André Gorz said, the transformation of the human being into consumer, worker, client, patient or functionary. In the process, like Mr Stevens, the butler in novelist Kazuo Ishiguro's *The Remains of the Day*, we forego even our most essential features. 'A butler of any quality', Mr Stevens thought, 'must be seen to *inhabit* his role, utterly and fully'; he cannot cast it aside as if 'it were nothing more than a pantomime costume'.

We do not even question the market's rationality and the new dependencies and forms of domination that it entails. Concerned only about performance, skills and image, we do not bother to think about the ends they serve. You 'put one brick upon another, add a third, and then a fourth', poet Philip Larkin reflected rather woefully, and you are not even giving yourself the time to 'wonder whether what you do has any worth'.

The odious absurdity of the means employed to attain the ends we so earnestly claim to pursue, the fatuity of a life committed to ends that defeat life itself, is ignored or, indeed, celebrated. We have, or we think we have, all the answers to questions we no longer remember. Life seems, indeed, to be an ever-unfolding tragic farce encapsulated in this old German advertisement which advised men: 'Smoke good and pure tobacco every day and you'll have no doctors' bills to pay.' The monstrous, the ludicrous, the perilous seem to be conditions to which we are only too happy to submit. Madness seems to be a liability indispensable to existence, inescapable, inevitable and yet conditional in our interaction with the world.

'Let me tell you,' Ivan says in *The Brothers Karamazov*, 'the absurd is only too necessary on earth.' Giacometti's figures, naked nerve patterns, Paul Klee's 'little scrawls', Magritte's juxtapositions of the ordinary and the ridiculous, or Francis Bacon's portraits hinting at mutilation or deformity suggestive of disintegration of the social being, all make the same point just as eloquently as despondently. Despairing of our era, Italian poet Primo Levi, an Auschwitz survivor, turned his eyes mockingly to heaven: 'Give us something to destroy,' he pleaded, 'give us something to deface, give us something to rape, give us something that burns, offends, cuts, smashes, fouls and makes us feel that we exist.'

The kind of society we live in, R. D. Laing, the Scottish psychiatrist, exploded, is one which systematically 'drives people out of their minds' – insanity, thus, is a perfectly rational adjustment to an insane world. To be normal, one has to be desensitised, live a life suitable to, and desired by, the socially engineered reality, behave according to its rules and conform with social roles. One has, indeed, to create a false self able to adapt to the artificiality of modern living. The system depends on it for its survival. Trying to achieve the personal transformation that would allow the emergence of one's true self and the expression of one's real needs is ridiculed. All honour is reserved, instead, as Friedrich Nietzsche once remarked, for petrified opinions, that prized collection of burnt-out light-bulbs. Laing's rebelliousness, in tune with that of his time, stirred up passions and engendered an atmosphere as boisterous as one might expect in a Saturday night mice cabaret held for the benefit of the town's cats and their wives.

But nothing much has changed. Theory, whether psychological, social or political, moved into action with the ferocity of nails as they grow upon fingers. In an apocalyptic vision of the future, an exasperated Michel Foucault, that great French thinker, did, thus, predict the end of it all. The world, he said, 'is near its final catastrophe.' But 'victory is neither God's nor the Devil's. It belongs to Madness'. Guided by an Ego devoid of any content, the latter reigns over whatever is bad in man. Madness, Foucault said fiercely, is not linked to the world and its subterranean forms but 'to man, to his weaknesses, dreams, and illusions ... It is man who constitutes madness in the attachment he bears to himself and by the illusions he entertains ... the imaginary relation he maintains with himself.'

Self-interest, sanctified in sacred rites by vanity and her eminently vile sisters, stupidity, avarice and envy, takes priority over any other concern. The whole, just like the stars which city-dwellers never see, seems no longer to exist. In its absence, in the vacuum created by what Hermann Broch, the German novelist, called 'inertia of feeling', there is no sense of shared purpose and joint responsibility, either. Good is what is good for 'me', 'me' being the individual, the corporation, the class, 'our' nation, race, religion, civilisation or whatever we happen to identify with. Responsibility, obviously, ends where claims to self-interest begin. 'Hating', Martial, the epigrammatist, said nearly two millenniums ago, 'is more economical than giving.' But alienated from the whole, man vanishes into inconsequentiality, while the whole, broken into its constituent parts, dematerialises. The free choice of the individual then lies, as Aldous Huxley put it, between insanity and lunacy. Adhering to the dream of a world that makes sense seems to be the prerogative of the unhinged – the 'anarchist', the 'nihilist', the 'madman', all of them nevertheless children of McWorld and its demeaned culture.

But the system, whether agreeable or not, is not separate from us. Its materialistic goals, receding like the horizon line and never reached, are our goals. Its insatiable needs, which are never met for they never end, are our needs; and its greed, which devours everything of non-monetary value, is our craving for more, presumed to mean better, which destroys the very thing that matters in life – life itself. 'Ours' is also 'their' indifference to whatever happens to the Other, whether the Other is aspects of our own selves, our fellow human beings, the non-human world, values, truth or objectivity. In the complacent postmodernist world in which we live, none of these is any of our concern. Nothing of the kind is mentioned in *The Comfortable Times*. The madness of the system, reflecting our own unbalanced priorities which recreate reality in a bubble, is, therefore, in the blood of our culture, the 'culture of the disinherited' as Raymond Williams, the British Marxist thinker called it, that gives the jaundiced colour to all pleasures, 'theirs' and 'ours'.

This is a situation from which we cannot disassociate ourselves. Consciousness and material reality, inner and outer, man and his Gods are not separate entities. They are, instead, aspects of the whole, transcending themselves, coming into being through each other, and transforming the whole of which they are parts. The system is not the Other, something external to our own selves and our own assumptions, values and expectations which our culture both reflects and defines. It neither can be nor is 'them', the conglomerates of wealth and power as opposed to all the rest of us, the decent human beings. It is 'us', all of us 'who', as Alexander Pope put it, 'gain'd no title, and who lost no friend', whose inner ideograms and confusions are externalised and projected outwards into the world only to be reflected backwards to us. At the root of everything, the early Marx pointed out, is man, the humans with all their constructive and destructive capabilities. Indeed, Henry Miller added, the trouble with man is man himself, his pride, his prejudices, his stupidity, his arrogance, his own petty, circumscribed view of life.

Hence Justice, denied by an aggressive system in all its dealings with the world, is also denied by the individual; and madness reigns supreme. 'Abandon every hope, ye who enter here', the inscription above Hell's gate informs the new arrivals, Dante tells us. The same announcement might just as well stay over the gates of the 21st century.

The search for 'truth', therefore, the postmodernists' 'prime Western illusion', needs necessarily to continue. But rather than an intellectual exercise carried out by postmodernist thinkers skilful enough to turn anything into something really incomprehensible, it is a challenge. To meet it, we need more than the blessings of 'virtual', 'surgical', 'digital' and even 'zero-casualty' wars, meetings of the G8 to stimulate economic growth, the illusory panacea for all ills, or violence in the streets of the First World. It demands more than either religious outrages, apocalyptic security or gestures of goodwill of the kind the multinationals make to placate the conscientious consumer. It takes also more than 'pity' and 'compassion' for the 'unfortunate'. Giving them money and bread may help, as novelist Isabel Allende would have said, to 'remove all guilt, cleanse the conscience, and alleviate nervous ailments'. It is not nevertheless a substitute for Justice. It also takes more than institutional reforms.

Confrontational, yet from a democratic rather than a Jihadic point of view, the children of McWorld have challenged global capitalism's practices and values as much as they have US President George W. Bush's Global War On Terror. But what also needs to be challenged are our own practices and values. To get through we need something more than a readjustment of IMF policies and fairness in world trade or stop-the-war campaigns. Cleaning the spiders out of the bath means dealing with a bankrupt culture, personified in its extreme, not just by Enron, the energy giant which contributed most generously to the corruption of the age, but also by that Athenian taxi driver who, after berating the politicians for their greed, rapaciousness and avarice, charged me twice the fare he should have.

Change, in other words, cannot be achieved in a society consisting of egotistic, disconnected, self-seeking individuals, full of themselves. It is, indeed, unattainable in a world of moral absolutes that always go hand-in-hand with 'guilt-neutralisation techniques' designed to lift the burden of conscience and help the bowels ease themselves. No society can resist the top executives' culture of greed if it is itself in the grip of such a culture, as no country can be better than the individuals who constitute it. Aristotle made the point early enough, at a time that making a point was not as hopeless as it is today. Conversely, no individual can have an incentive to act decently if his or her society is genetically engineered to fail its better self and programmed to self-destruct. Decency cannot be legislated.

Following the events of September the 11th in the year of the big wind, the dream of a better world receded into the background – the events 'changed everything'. The United States, one-eyed like a lighthouse, without any sense of perspective, split the universe between those who are with 'us', presumably the 'axis of good', and those who are with the 'terrorists', the 'axis of evil' which deserves fully our perfected looks of disgust. Lumped in with the terrorists were all those who oppose the imperious reach of US economic, political and military power. But, equally true, and though the world is running so fast that it cannot be caught even by its own shadow, nothing has ever changed. The battle between Good and Evil, watched by God from the shores of eternity for free, is still being waged albeit with less ferocity but with the same gusto as in Tamerlane's times.

The institutionalised madness which, in the name of Reason, has turned the colour of this world 'like last year's seaweed', has nothing to do with Reason. It is, instead, the apotheosis of Unreason leading both and simultaneously, as Max Weber, the German sociologist, decried, to the rationalisation and the disenchantment of the world, or, as James Joyce put it, to the 'general paralysis of the insane'.

Their views were shared by the giants of contemporary literature. They all stood against the madness of the time, the outcome of the pyrrhic victory of the Ego, 'the tomb', as the anonymous mystical poet has said, 'of every hope'. Yet, madness, 'the daughter of Night' in Greek mythology, still sits in the driver's seat without a map, the map of hope, which has been mislaid in the alleys of our contortions and misinterpretations.

Pandora, a most beautiful woman Zeus sent to punish mankind for its arrogance, opened the jar which Zeus had given her as a gift – the jar of sorrows. Work, old age, sickness, insanity and vice plagued the world in no time. Hope alone remained in the jar, and Hope dissuaded mankind from committing suicide. But this was, apparently, not meant to happen. Hence at a time that man's destructive capabilities have galloped far ahead of his wisdom, and the 'Doomsday Clock' tells us we are only two minutes from our midnight appointment with apocalypse, we are frantically trying to let Hope, too, out of the box. This may well be the assessment of a man faithful to his prejudices, out of key, as Ezra Pound might say, with his time or common sense. But a common sense that can accommodate a re-energised economic, religious and political fundamentalism, and extremist acts such as that horrendous attack on the US and the ferocious American reaction to it, has nothing much to recommend itself for.

Part I: The Culture

1. To Be is to Need

At times I wonder whether I perhaps live in the outer suburbs of reality, in a pseudo-intellectual enclave, cosy, smug and condescending, intolerant of common sense, arrogant in its presumptions. I think of our world as being fragmented as a broken mirror, as perverse as fighting for a place in the hell-express, as bland as a portion of Kentucky Fried Chicken. What I think is out there is a mad, mad, mad world. But it is exactly this understanding of reality, so preposterous, that makes me think that, after all, my assumptions may be as wrong as the planetesimal hypothesis. Perhaps the madness, if there is a madness, is only inside my head and what I see, probably from an outpost located in the day's far-west where only sunsets are detailed, is not reality itself, but only its distorted image.

The fact is that in the world we live in, 'everything', as Mayakovsky, the Russian poet rather scornfully testified, 'is in such terrifying order, at rest, in its proper place.' Deaths, though not suicides as yet, are broadcast live on TV, the supermarkets are well-stocked with lots of things we can easily do without, the world's car-park has still plenty of room at the few places relatively free of mankind for expansion. We have an unprecedented availability of goods and services at affordable prices – New Zen Green Tea Truffles, ski holidays in Dubai, take away Thai food, virtual sex over the net, reproductions of Matisse as good as the originals, Giorgio Armani T-shirts or breast enlargements – 'the bustline you've always wanted.' There is almost nothing that a relatively humble amount of money cannot buy, nothing that the middle class will not consider itself entitled to have, hardly anything to complain about that the Trading Standards Authority cannot fix.

And, of course, everyone has a choice – the consumer choice

which is the naturalised citizen of the capitalist republic: plenty of obese Sunday newspapers ready, without the least provocation, to portray the trivial and inconsequential, an abundance of politicians who can prove conclusively that they are not tainted by any belief in anything, a plethora of heroes from the pop, movie or football world who can sign their name to contracts providing remunerations whose accent I can neither recognise nor comprehend.

Modern life has, of course, more to it than my cynicism would allow for. It offers much which I could not even dream of during my time as a kid. My parents had sent me to an expensive Athenian public school, which was a great privilege, but we really had nothing with which to heat our house in the cold winter days, no running hot water or a fridge, no proper cooking or bathing facilities, no telephone or, much less, a car. Incidentally, we did have a radio which, attracting Mr Spyros, my opera-loving neighbour, gave me a taste for Italian opera and some of the all-time greats – Caruso, Tito Gobbi and Chaliapin – which I might otherwise have never acquired.

Having made my acquaintance with deprivation in the course and the aftermath of Greece's long wars, I cannot, therefore, dismiss easily the benefits the consumer society provides. Nor can I look back to those times or even further back to the Middle Ages with the romantic attachment of the aristocratic opponents of industrialism or the neo-Luddite enthusiasm for a technology-free environment. I would rather take my washing to the laundrette than to the river bank, contact people by phone rather than through pigeons, and use a computer rather than a quill pen. Democratisation of consumption has bestowed on us many benefits that have not only made life much easier, but, if one is to be realistic about it all, we can no longer do without.

Yet this market-led world, which welcomes every infant as a potential customer, moving intrinsically towards maximisation, has something inherently insane about it. The fundamental law which determines, defines and delineates it demands constant growth seen as the only means to maintain and, hopefully, increase the players' market share. Fear of competition, of losses, of failure and collapse is the psychological force behind this drive. You just fail to grow, you are outgrown by your rivals, you perish. But fear goes here hand in hand with greed and the insatiable need for more because whatever we have is never good enough.

Hence we are flooded ceaselessly with new products: Kate Moss' style in Topshop clothes, Giorgio Armani 'fluid trousers' which 'reflect today's more informal attitudes', new, natural paints for 'a bright, healthy and sustainable future', BlackBerry Pearl smartphones with both 'looks and brains', Paul Smith designer ties to wear to the pub, new 'ultimate driving machines' ensuring 'high performance, low emissions, zero guilt', time zone chronographs that display the opening hours of the world's major stock markets, multimineral and multivitamin food supplements, exercise machines for all major abdominal muscles, Wonderbra shorts, multimedia PCs, trolley gas barbecues, solar-powered wristwatches, youth replenishing creams or hayfever microsprays. Before we have developed an intimate relationship with the 'old', we have new models of cars 'surprisingly roomy', with 'inner strengths', 'perfect lines' or 'quickclear heated windscreens', new Yves Saint Laurent shoes and Jean Paul Gaultier spectacle frames, new high speed PCs with 'the fastest ever Pentium processor', 'flexible investments', 'must-haves for him' or 'simple, safe and effective treatments of male impotence'. Just as soon as we managed to acquaint ourselves with e-mail, we had the blogs, and before we could even understand what e-commerce is, we were invited to greet the arrival of m-commerce.

The customer, appreciated by the free market economy as much as the fox used to be by the furrier, is eager to oblige and happy to acknowledge needs never before suspected. We buy silly things like barbecue-flavoured salt, tomato ketchup-flavoured crisps or Greek salad – 'just add lettuce' – and pies and pasties made from something called 'meat', the origins of which we dare not question . Cheap and unidentifiable raw materials, reformulated, permulated, coloured, flavoured, dehydrated, frozen and labelled 'food' end up on our shelves in fancy packaging, often more costly, and also more appetizing, than the contents. The fellow who no longer wanted cheap human food after he had accidentally tried dog food tells the story, not just of the food industry, but also of our culture.

The market is there to take care of everybody's needs. Particularly well-catered for are those customers whose sleep is disturbed by the rumble of personal memories still unreplaced by the collective ones produced on television. Within easy reach at the local supermarket they can confidently expect to find 'old time' whiskey, 'natural' mineral water, 'old fashioned' beer, or 'traditionally prepared' spaghetti sauces just like those their Italian mama used to make. The search for authenticity, embracing all possible objects of desire, has turned into a fully-blown obsession which the market is only too happy to meet.

It looks as if nothing can can be satisfied outside of the marketplace – not even our basic needs. We go places to be entertained because we can no longer entertain ourselves, we live on takeaways because we have no time to cook, we talk to people through the internet because our neighbourhood and community exist no longer. In the unpeopled environment of our crowded cities, we expect to be provided for in return for payment, and we assume that those paid to take care of us will do so better than ourselves. Ivan Illich, the Austrian philosopher and social critic, called this pervasive market culture a 'radical monopoly'. 'The establishment of radical monopoly', he said, 'happens when people give up their native ability to do what they can for themselves and for each other in exchange for something "better" that can be done for them.'

Rather than sing we, thus, buy CDs; rather than walk we use cars; rather than cook we microwave; rather than do our figures ourselves we give the job to an electronic calculator. Likewise, we do not paint – we buy, instead, reproductions. We do not exercise – we watch sports on television. We do not write – we email. Techno-addiction, fed ceaselessly by a bewildering variety of electronics, has made us both mentally and materially fully dependent on machines. With contempt for anything genuine, we are thrilled to let them turn the pages of our lives, happy to see, as a result, the departure of both the natural skills with which we are endowed and the pleasures that derive from their exercise. The day that cyberspace provides sexual gratification will undoubtedly be heralded as the day of liberation from cumbersome personal interactions and independence from the burden of relationships.

The total dependence on machines and fleets of specialists, those feted for knowing more and more about less and less, does not seem to bother us. Presumably, rather than the mark of our vulnerability, it is the mark of our sophistication. Caught by the long arm of our illusions, we are sold to 'progress' and go unthinkingly for its products, feeding the locusts which have taken over our cities and our selves. Not surprisingly, even very personal needs are met in a businesslike manner in the marketplace. To find partners we place ads in the press, search the Net or seek the help of dating agencies. To do things outside our home we entrust our young children to child-minders – the family is no longer there to take care of them. To get the support one would expect to receive from friends we go to psychotherapists. Listening is a career now.

Capitalist logic, with its 'red veins full of money', creates, as Austro-French philosopher André Gorz stated, the greatest possible number of needs to be satisfied with the largest possible amount of marketable goods and services in order to derive the greatest possible profit from the greatest possible flow of energy and resources. It is this logic, underpinned by a belief that the humans have an infinite number of needs, that has become our culture's assumption, its bodiless voice, the force behind the drive for more and more which, it is assumed, means only one thing: better.

Hence the assumption of 'all good people, husbands to one's wife' and all the rest of us is that *to be is to need*, and, as the market never ceases to offer, we never cease to need. That emphatic and uncompromising advertisement by *Orange*, the mobile phone network, simply underlines this fundamental cultural assumption. 'All deserve more', it informed us, meaning, not only that more is better, but also that we are all entitled to more and better. Like Erysichthon, the man who had been punished by the Goddess Demeter to suffer perpetual hunger irrespective of how much he ate because he had refused to stop cutting down sacred trees to build a new banqueting hall, we can never satisfy our hunger for more.

We buy pieces of equipment which are practically out of date before we learn how to use them, are made to be enjoyed for a lifetime but last as long as the English summer, and yet we need them as much as, to paraphrase the radical feminist slogan, a fish needs a bicycle. We acquire remote controls so that we do not have to do anything manually and items to keep fit because we do not do anything manually. We buy comfortable furniture or therapy time to find the peace of mind to deal with our collapsing personal world and at the same time we make commitments that destroy both our peace of mind and our personal world. We get cars, microwaves or interactive refrigerators, i.e. capable of talking to our oven, to make the best use of our limited time and spend the day working hard to buy cars, microwaves or interactive tools.

Speed is the essence of the time. Time is speed, how quickly things are done as if in a competition for the fastest watch in town. Hailed inadvertently early in the twentieth century by the futurists – Marinetti, Balla, Severini and others – as a liberation from the constraints of the past, speed, 'the roar and speed of a racing car', turned into the new moral religion: fast food, fast sex – a pair of spare knickers in the office drawer just in case, fast money, fast tanning, fast lines of communication, fast happiness on hallucinatory drugs, one-minute bedtime stories for the children. If you go for it, there is even 'ear piercing while U-wait', according to the window-sign of a Dublin beautician. The pace of everything is so fast that we only need to blink our eyes, filled, as Evelyn Waugh, the English social satirist, might say, with that 'gin-fogged look that is common to sailors and the secretaries of the great, and comes from too short sleep', to miss an entire new generation of Microsoft Windows. The only thing that still seems to take as much time as before is a woman's effort to find the car keys in her bag.

Instant-everything is the power which has forced us to move from our home in space to a new home, in time, in the infinite expanses of virtual reality. The shift relentlessly destroys all our connections with reflection, thought, contemplation, wisdom or substantiality. Unbelievable though it may sound, earlier times were not viewed all that differently. H.G. Wells, the English author of some of the earliest science-fiction novels, could not stand the 'pushful days' of his time – and it was still only 1901.

With all sorts of things available at somewhat affordable prices, life is, of course, much easier today. To deny it serves no purpose. Yet, the price that this market-led world, the phantasmagoria of nothingness, extracts for its favours is exorbitant, far in excess of what we should be willing, or can afford, to pay. Goods are produced and services become available to consumers not out of recognition of their needs as human beings, but for profit. Needs are, therefore, never accepted as needs if their satisfaction makes no one any money. Back in 1932, novelist Aldous Huxley published his *Brave New World*, a nightmare set in 'this year of stability, A.F. 632', i.e. 632 years after Ford manufactured his first car, the famous Model T, by mass-production methods. 'Imagine', the director of the Central London Hatchery and Conditioning Centre tells his students, 'the folly of allowing people to play elaborate games which do nothing whatever to increase consumption. It's madness.'

Love between two people is not recognised as a need because no one makes money out of it. But the exploitation of sex for profit, though it leads to the desexualisation of the body and the sexualisation of the brain, is definitely a 'need' to be satisfied in a thousand ways – 'more sex for your money', reads the ad for *The Erotic Review*. Likewise, we were invited to 'eat football, sleep football (and) drink Coca Cola', as the tasteless slogan of the soft drinks world empire encouraged us to do, but not as participants in the game; no profits in that. We were invited, instead, as pathetic paying spectators. Or as readers: 'There is more to life than watching sport', *The Guardian* newspaper tells us; 'Read about it as well.'

What has no price has no value, and it does not feature in the pages of *Which?* magazine, the full-time consumer's bible. Spring water from the Highlands is of value because we can buy it in bottles at the local supermarket, but clean air is of no value because nobody has found the way as yet to sell it to us in plastic containers. Likewise, human relations are of value when a professional is paid to facilitate them, but of no value to a society consisting of individuals who care only about their own selves. The system has no time or energy to invest in what is outside the flow of money, and institutional power has no interest in it. Technology, for its part, in spite of its sophisticated 'communication' systems, has given communication between people all the rope it needs to hang itself. Power, assessing everything in terms of costs and benefits for itself, has turned into a vandal.

In the throes of a hectic life, we no longer need to think what we want. Those plotting the happiness of mankind do it for us. They tell us relentlessly of the unfulfilled parts of our existence and urge us to seek fulfilment in the world of commodities, find in this world, as in Chrysler's new PT Cruiser, an 'emotional rescue' from the stress the world of commodities creates for our benefit. 'Suddenly therapy', the Chrysler ad tells us, 'doesn't seem the answer at all' – for the answer buy a car. What is being offered is a shortcut to happiness, retail therapy. You can make 'all your dreams come true' just by borrowing money from Abbey National, 'liberate the imagination' by opening an account with the Royal Bank of Scotland, 'know who you are' by owning a Peugeot 406. You can 'get a new face' by having a glass of dry Martini, discover the 'real way to true enlightenment' by driving a Citroen or 'vote yourself to power' by switching to Virgin for gas and electricity. It is like prescribing Latin as a cure for arthritis. But for the advertising industry, the blabarians of our time, it works.

Its omnifarious pledges, with glances filled with sweet promises, fill a gap in life and open the road to 'self-actualisation' which provides an ethical dimension to the consumer economy. Consumers feel compelled to buy and use the products even when they see the manipulation at work and are able to sustain a critical distance from what is on offer.

Yet, we depend on consumer goods to escape the twitching agony of an existence lost in the streets of triviality, to get some pleasure in a world unwilling to give us any outside the market context, to furnish the empty, untenanted space within. Even consuming green teas, Jacob Weisberg, editor of Slate.com, tells us, makes a Californian feel 'not just spiritually complete, but a morally superior being', at one with the universe and in peace with himself. The substantiality, individuality, certainty and popularity these products ostensibly provide, this grandiloquous nonsense as Lake poet Robert Southey might say, are all things denied to us by the power of our impersonality and the poverty of interpersonal relations. The same promises compensate materially for an emotionally underprivileged life, an underdeveloped personality, social alienation, boredom or lack of self-esteem. This is true particularly in the case of brands which turn into the main source of solace and comfort.

Brands, as Young & Rubicam, one of the world's biggest advertising agencies, declared, are 'the new religion', representing a set of beliefs, a set of values to live by, a way to get a life. Approvingly, James B. Twitchell in his book *Lead Us Into Temptation*, explained: the triumph of American materialism gives us a profound source of meaning, purpose, and joy – the joy of ownership. More importantly, through the purchase and possession of things, we define ourselves, establish our identity, make our statement to others, claim our place in society and validate our existence. We do not have lives, Twitchell happily concluded, we have lifestyles. But this is what we want. In the frozen featurelessness of our time, the heart seems to beat no longer: the existential chronometer has stopped functioning or we have stopped existing. We are happy to embrace a culture which finds nothing wrong with plastic trees or values, because, partly, anything else looks like an abandoned dog wandering aimlessly in the heat of the day.

In *Art and Eros*, Iris Murdoch, the Irish-born British philosopher and novelist, has Socrates say that 'good art tells us more truth about our lives and our world than any other kind of thinking or speculation.' Assuming this is true, the state of our art is a damning indictment of our culture. Assessed only in terms of their commercial potential, mass appeal, ratings and charts, the arts of the twentieth century – film, television and pop music – 'a sub-department of marketing', as Eric Hobsbawm, the British Marxist historian, said, sell thrills, sentimentality and feelgood stories. Good is what attracts the most attention and sells, not what challenges society – and art that does not make 'virtue adorable and vice repugnant', which is how Diderot, the moral philosopher and apostle of the Enlightenment put it, or at least does not challenge society, is not art.

This commodities' civilisation cuts so deep that it leaves nothing unaffected. When the black man sings 'when I get to heaven there's no one there to turn me out', when the Greens remonstrate 'they took all the trees and put them in a tree museum and charged all people a dollar and a half just to see them', when 'the real nowhere man (is) sitting in his nowhere land making all his nowhere plans for nobody' it all ends up as great entertainment – we all enjoy Ella Fitzgerald, Joni Mitchell or John Lennon and Paul McCartney. Like the trout, so voracious it can devour anything it can grab, the market can consume anything to sustain its monstrosity.

Pop music has become an extension of the advertising and corporate entertainment industry, and so have sports, cultural institutions or 'celebrities' associated with 'good causes' which are associated with products. Even the New Agers – those who like their sex weak and their barleycup strong – fall into the trap: they denounce the materialism of the free market culture only to end up as the counter-culture's consumers of supposedly spiritual and environmentally-friendly services or products. The Mind,

Body, Spirit exhibition held annually in London, though it attracts exhibitors and visitors disillusioned with current values, is perhaps a good example of the failure to establish an alternative to commodity culture. The alternative is not an alternative if all it does is substitute on its shelves Chanel *eau de cologne* with aromatic oils, for what has to be denied is the constant creation of new needs and the dependence on what is provided.

The alternative is not an alternative, either, when New Age apostle Deepak Chopra, the Indian-born American who would never make a bank deposit without reciting his 'seven spiritual laws', continues to call for the fulfilment of the impossible capitalist dream. The means to this end, supposedly spiritual, are different. The goal is, however, the same: the enhancement, as Chopra said, of 'your ability to create unlimited wealth with effortless ease' [sic]. A grave with a view is presumably then well-deserved. Rampant commercialism, even if it sells reincarnation insurance policies rather than life assurance, is, if not more, at least as offensive as that of the Old Age. It hurts the culture of greed as much as Xerxes, the fifth century BC Persian king, hurt the sea of the Hellespont when, in punishment, he branded it with hot irons.

There is, of course, nothing wrong with enjoying the small 'luxuries' of life, which, Peter Kropotkin, the Russian father of anarcho-communism, once said, are as human as the dreams of a more fulfilling life. They are all necessary to survive an afternoon 'entirely taken up with toothache and low spirits' or break the monotony of a life 'wicked', as English poet Wendy Cope put it, 'as a ginless tonic and wild as pension plans'.

Myself, I love watching the latest world-disaster movie in which a looming catastrophe is safely arrested by Arnold Schwarzenegger, the Governor of California, whose name, like mine, seems to be a punishment for a past life misdemeanour. I am taken by Arsenal's Cesc Fabregas, when he cleverly tricks the opposition, and enjoy a glass of ouzo in the honey-gold serenity of an Aegean summer afternoon. But I refuse to be caught in the commodity culture's web of subliminal influences, to measure quality of life by the level of commodity consumption. I reject the 'needs' I am told I have, the commodities which, transformed by packaging, advertising and marketing, provide me with a lifestyle.

The fantasy world that the commodification of our existence represents, those 'huge heaps of littleness around', is the means of our self-deception, the foundation on which our illusions rest. If and when business refuses to take responsibility for the effect of services or products they offer – the 'let the consumer decide' policy – that is also the measure of our amorality. 'The fatness of our pursy times' can accommodate anything, even the knife that cuts life through.

Yet whatever the circumstances, unlike dreams which can sometimes be fulfilled, needs are never satisfied even if the government is to tax a city for us, as Herodotus says it did, to ensure a good supply of slippers for the Persian queen. We do not know when to say enough is enough, for in the kind of world we live, enough is never enough even if it is more than we can use. Dazzled by the eloquence of their promises, there are always new products we 'need' to acquire, new technological openings we 'need' to explore, and enticing lifestyles we 'need' to go for if we are to get full value for our illusionary uniqueness, the creator's present to the world for the rarest of occasions. 'You have everything', pantheist Nicaraguan poet Rubén Darío cried almost in despair, 'except one thing: God!' His poem *To Roosevelt*, written in 1904, was, of course, an outraged condemnation of the US interventionist policies in 'our America', 'the Catholic America, Spanish America'.

Needs never met destroy the social fabric of any given society. Plato made the point in *Politeia* in a way that leaves hardly any room for comfort. In the pursuit of his needs, a man, he wrote, enters into debts and mistreats his parents before turning to crime to raise money. People like him 'steal, break into houses, cut purses, snatch cloaks, plunder temples, and kidnap people for the slave-trade. Some, if they are good at speaking, become sycophants, false witnesses, takers of bribes' or, perhaps, executives of Enron, Andersen and WorldCom. In what turned into a classic account of the origins of *coups d'état*, these people, Plato held, when numerous enough, helped along by people's stupidity, would turn to a leader who, encountering resistance, would maltreat his motherland as much as he once mistreated his own mother. If he could, he would maltreat, indeed, the entire world. The connection between the personal and the political evident in Plato's thesis is, however, bound to excite as much interest as a proposal to turn an OECD report into a movie.

Marx talked in his time about the 'fetishisation of commodities'. In our need-conditioned days, and although sociologists would say that we are creatures of desires rather than needs, one can also talk about the fetishisation of needs. We need our needs and we do not even think that there is anything wrong with them. In the same way, Hieron's wife never thought that there was anything wrong with her husband's bad breath because she assumed all men smelled the same.

'Nausea', Yannis Ritsos, the poet, interpreting our unvoiced soliloquies, ventured to suggest, 'is not an illness. It's an answer.'

2. Even Eternity is Too Short

Presumed equal, we all have the same right to feast on fish and chips on the Northern Line or enjoy a glass of Salmanazar Möet & Chandon champagne at the Ritz Hotel in Paris. But as only very few can afford the Salmanazar at the Ritz Hotel, the rest of us are there only to prove that, as a result, equality is an illusion. The fact is that there is no way we can all have the same. Capitalism, or indeed any other system, cannot give everyone the mansion of a Venetian ambassador, a holiday in the Caribbean, a villa in the South of France, a Porsche, a Modigliani, a yacht, a Ph.D. or Imelda

Marcos' shoe collection.

Nature's lottery, in the first place, has distributed unequally the various natural assets. Some are endowed with more intelligence or wisdom, physical strength, energy, imagination, stamina, persistence, presence, natural skills, drive, ambition or better looks, which are often the wild card in a person's destiny, than others. Although all equal in our nakedness or loneliness, not everyone can be a Hegel, a Buster Keaton or an Angelina Jolie, beautiful, rich and famous. This kind of inequality, implicit in the demands for equality of opportunity which ensures that the satisfaction of some of them will lessen inequality, cannot be questioned except by the mean-spirited. It is in nature and, no matter what we do, nature cannot be trained. A stone, Aristotle said, cannot be habituated to rise, however often we may try to train it by throwing it into the air.

Yet the effort to be 'somebody', in terms understood by a market culture dismissive of remote meanings and contumacious of anything that cannot be measured, never ends. For, the unobtainable, the untried pleasures of a fancied lifestyle, all things society tells us are worth having, seem to be tantalisingly both within and beyond our reach. Oblivious to all things money cannot buy we, thus, subscribe to the axioms of the system and run to arrive quicker than quick to an arrival point which does not exist. 'In love with a particular life (we) haven't got', as Philip Larkin put it, we never have enough. Sheep, feeding on grass, take as much as they need to live. Man never has enough. A naked young woman is never naked enough. 'Unlimited wealth' remains the dream which even New Age guru Deepak Chopra, rather than censure, endorses in the context of his ludicrous spirituality. His understanding of a fulfilling life, uninspired by love beyond the self, is as impressive as the shine left behind by a snail. It does not close any weary distances.

Having less, or just what is necessary for a dignified life, seems to run irreverently against the grain of some cosmic masterplan. 'I had nothing, yet was not poor', said the poet in Goethe's *Faust* – the notion, outdated, seems to represent today only the cravings

29

of yesterday abandoned at the disused bridge to meaning. Having less is, presumably, the denial of our right to be happy and gleam deservedly like a white stone in the rain, to obtain or maintain the 'uniqueness' and 'individuality' acquisitions are supposed to confer upon us. It disables us, Jacques Lacan, the French reinterpreter of Freudian psychoanalysis, explained, from acquiring more than the other with whom we compare or identify ourselves.

Jean Baudrillard, the French postmodernist thinker, took the point a bit further. Goods, he said, are not produced to satisfy irreducible primary needs. In the unconscious structure of social relations they are treated, instead, as the signifiers of our position in society – the realm of necessity is left behind. Consumption does not, therefore, homogenise; it does, instead, differentiate through the sign system, and sustains what Freud called 'the narcissism of small differences'. Yet the perceived needs remain, uniting us in the pursuit of more, more of the same, the artificial stimulant for both continuous 'progress' and endless discontent which continues to call for the impossible. Their timely satisfaction, before the neighbours find out we have not got what they already have, is just as important.

Thorstein Veblen, the American social scientist, had made the point much earlier when he talked about what he called 'conspicuous consumption', the effort to keep up with the crowd and impress with our financial power and status. The principle has not lost its validity over the years. As a Rover advertisement reassured us rather disenchantingly, 'more extras make a better impression'. But 'extras' cost money – everything in Rome has its price.

Hence money is the cultural foundation of our world, the condition of capitalist development, the flag of a system which, as Lorca said, 'has never fought, and never will fight, for heaven'. It is also the measure of our worth, the means to achieve recognition as people of some standing and the force that underpins our self-respect, even the feeling of being valued as human beings. It means success. And success, this middle class aphrodisiac, is expected to give us, the children of the great material expansion, all that is considered worth having: wealth and all that money can buy. Well into the fourth year of Tony Blair's 'Third Way', journalist Nigella Lawson wrote in *The Observer*: 'It's hard to think of a way of life uncontaminated by the acquisitionist fantasy.' To exist, or to be thought worthy of existing, 'a comfortable amount of spending power' is necessary; 'without that, you're nothing'. She could have said the same another few years later as the system and, rather more depressingly, our proclivity tells us, in a language good enough even for Tarzan to understand, that we need money to be happy except that, miserably, the money we earn is never good enough to make us happy. 'The blanket', as Günter Grass, the German novelist said, 'is always too short.'

Yet our aspirations, conditioned, tend always to live above their income. It could not have been otherwise, for anything different is bound to conflict with the colours of our hyperactive, and yet so disenchanting, daily routines, the purity of our decline. Hence our values unroll on the quintessential script of the moneyed infinitesimal wisdom. They are assessed in exclusively monetary terms articulated in the coarse voice of cash, loud enough to raise the dead and kill the living. Payment, as Carlyle, the nineteenth century Scottish historian and political philosopher, said, remains 'the sole nexus' between people, which explains why capitalism has the survival skills of a woman living off her talents. It also explains why we have ended up as part-time humans.

Nothing, as a result, from forests to human dignity, from wild life to freedom, or from pollution-free cities to tradition, has a right to exist if this right impedes the creation of 'unlimited wealth', which, kindly, Barclays Bank has offered to manage under the slogan: 'Protect your wealth, grow it, use it and pass it on.' But 'taking no limit as the limit', as Aeschines, the fourth century BC Athenian statesman, said, 'is for each man his Fury, bidding him to cut the throat of his fellow-citizens, to become a tyrant's henchman, to help overthrow democracy.' It is madness, but madness has become our way of life protected by law; and ugliness, in a secret

31

pact with a Reason as ugly as ugliness itself, has taken over our lives. In its chamber of horrors, Wesley Clark, NATO's Supreme Commander, commands thus his men to 'degrade, disrupt, devastate and destroy' Serbia, and President George W. Bush launches his 'shock and awe' military strike on Iraq that shocked the world and awed the Americans.

Ivan Illich called this unstoppable crusade for more 'the modernisation of poverty'. By endlessly recreating scarcity in order to recreate inequality and hierarchy, he said, capitalist society gives rise to more unfulfilled needs than it satisfies. The growth rate of frustration exceeds largely that of material wealth, denying, thus, as Democritus astutely remarked in the fifth century BC, the present and all the good things it offers.

The issue has nothing to do with the elimination of poverty, which may or may not be achieved, but with a society which has not alleviated – and never will – the relative poverty it harbours. For poverty, as opposed to destitution which is definable, is a relative condition: it involves comparisons – an Afghan with an automobile may consider himself well off whereas an American with an automobile may well consider himself poor. As such, it relates to only one thing, the exclusion of the individual from the dominant lifestyle which is by definition never that of the majority. What makes people poor is their inability to obtain what their society defines as 'good'. Poor, André Gorz said, are those 'less well-off in relation to the sociocultural standard that directs and stimulates desires'. In this sense, poverty, built into the one-dimensionality of the system, will never disappear even if ham-coloured Americans decide to carry out war on it with nuclear weapons. People, never satisfied, will never cease to strive for more and better, both defined in terms of what money can buy. And whatever money can buy is never good enough.

One may be able to fly to the Maldives for a short break, but he or she will also, if wealthy enough, need an aeroplane seat in a row which is separated from the one in front by 55 inches rather than 31.

A limousine as big as a jumbo jet with 'elbowroom on Salisbury Plain' for ground transportation is also a must. The growing army of the new rich – investment bankers, privatised companies' executives, corporation lawyers, jackpot entrepreneurs, property developers, media and advertising moguls or stars of the entertaining world, from actors to pop singers and footballers – together with the old rich, will never settle for anything less. What they buy with their money is privilege – the personal care and attention provided by sales people who hover tactfully and offer advice, doormen who carry their luggage, hoteliers who address them respectfully as befits their elevated status, secretaries who arrange their business and social engagements to which they are to be chauffeured.

They all, of course, also have their personal trainers, masseurs, personal assistants, beauticians, therapists, chefs, decorators, planners, financial advisers, life coaches, managers of their spiritual affairs or people employed to polish the firewood and straighten the pictures in their mansions. Whatever they do, the rich, new or old, are within their rights as much as I was when I went cruising on a Bangkok river in a hired boat photographing the destitute locals living in shanties on its shores. But all I felt, incidentally, was embarrassment for being there as the representative of a system which grants the right to dignity only to those who can afford to pay for it.

Exclusivity and distinctive consumption are bound to remain the prerogatives of the rich, for as soon as the object of desire reaches the shelves of the mass-market the rich make sure they find other ways to re-establish their positional superiority. The car, which used to be a status symbol when the vast majority of people could not afford to buy one, has become a nuisance in our days, and holidaying in Torremolinos and Benidorm, a sign of one's elevated position in society when air travel was prohibitive for the masses, is now the working class' holiday destination. The rich will not go to places where, as George Seferis, the poet, says, 'the waves are drowned in the noise from the radio'. They will never end a nameless number on a faceless list to be afterwards mislaid, like Boris Pasternak's Lara.

Indeed the dream-world the free market always promises, and always denies, degenerates rapidly into a nightmare the moment ordinary people can have access to it. Equality, like ordinary ugliness or cruelty, is intolerable for the rich – it abolishes distinction, which is the reward of their riches. As W.S. Gilbert, the Victorian librettist, put it succinctly, 'when everyone is somebody, no-one is anybody.' There is no pleasure in driving a Porsche if everyone you know has got one, or flying for a quick *Einspaänner* with sweet *Mehlspeisse* in Vienna's *Griensteidl on Michaelerplatz* if everybody else can also do the same.

Defined by these criteria, the new poor of our days, those with a degree from Westminster University and a two-bedroom flat in Clapham Common, have to come to terms with a life not as privileged as they might have expected. They have to live with the indignity of spelling their names for the benefit of the season rail ticket officer, queue at Marks & Spencer to pay for the jumper they bought, and deal with automated and digitized services rather than humans.

Personal services, too expensive to run for the benefit of the new poor, are bound to become as outdated as the door-to-door milkman – what will remain are personalised services for the wealthy. At the same time, the middle class, those who once thought they had arrived, are rapidly being transformed into the servants of the super-rich – just since 1990, the US has seventy-six per cent more physical therapists, forty percent more gardeners, thirty-nine percent more restaurant cooks and hotel personnel. The middle class does not like this new social divide. It does not think it is funny. It is rather difficult, indeed, to see the funny side of it especially if it does not exist.

That was the case in Greece back in the 1980s, when an all-round incoherence was looking in vain for a mother. The 'socialists', in their effort to overcome Marxist class definitions, ingeniously divided the people between 'privileged' and 'non-privileged'. Their construct looked, naturally, like a sophomoric joke for no Greek would ever place himself among the 'privileged' lot, for, irrespective of how much one earned, there was always someone else bound to earn more. 'Clearly', Sylvia Plath said, 'the genius of plenitude houses himself elsewhere.' Having all accorded themselves the status of the 'non-privileged', and also the right to blame those 'privileged' for their own lesser status, they subsequently set their eyes on somehow less illustrious goals. Stupidity and greed then reduced the limitless to finite. Even eternity was too short.

The new egalitarianism, rather than being based on respect for the rights of human beings, was founded on their total disrespect – we were all equals by default, because nobody, whatever his or her merit, deserved, or was entitled to, anything. The rancorous lumpenbourgeoisie, in particular, loved to blame because, although its disesteemed members had enough to be happy, they did not feel happy. Life was not fair – they were born barefoot, they had to breathe the polluted air their own cars produced and live with people like themselves. And they were not even aware of their predicament. Wickedness, as Plato said, can never know either itself or excellence.

Striving for 'more and better' has, however, nothing to do with our right to happiness. It is, instead, the offspring of a nightmare helped to life by greed, this sickening feeling activated, as I read somewhere, in the region of the brain called the anterior insular cortex, and also envy, which Bertrand Russell chillingly described as 'the basis of democracy'. Greed, never in plain clothes, acknowledges only one objective: the effortless accumulation of riches. The tone is set here by the fat cats, those who, like Philoxenus, pray that their throat might become longer than a crane's to enjoy the wealth they grab and the intangible assets which belong to society as a whole. Their hard-boiled ethos has produced a culture you would think twice before inviting for dinner, yet opposition to it remains ineffective.

Envy has received much less attention than greed. Its theory, as a result, though built on a large plot, has plenty of space for improvements. The power of envy, the universal envy that breeds greed, was acknowledged by Marx himself, who saw in it the essence of the antisocial competition between individuals. For Nietzsche vengeful feelings, the hatred for 'noble values', express only the spiteful 'slave morality' of 'the herd'. Emotions of envy, spite, hatred and revenge, Scheler likewise claimed, are the expression of the 'common man's' repressed human nature. Inherent in our nature, a 'constitutional factor' that points to the limitations of both therapy and politics, envy unleashes destructive impulses, and in the innate conflict between good and evil, right and wrong, love and hatred, it accentuates the negative in our nature. Adorno and Horkheimer, the early theorists of the Frankfurt School, in their critique of the Enlightenment, insisted that 'the dark impulse' is the predominant force in human nature.

It was Freud, however, who placed envy, the feeling that reveals itself in the syphilitic's proneness of infecting other people, in the centre of the debate. Claims for justice and equality, he said, are rooted in the repressed initial envy, 'the penis envy' – for Melanie Klein, the Austrian-born psychoanalyst, they are rooted in the infant's primary envy of all that its mother possesses, her breasts, and in the ensuing uncontrollable greedy and destructive fantasies. Freud made the point powerfully in his re-evaluation of the Biblical story of the woman who inadvertently crushed her babyson and then exchanged the dead body for the living one of her friend. To resolve the dispute, King Solomon asked for a sword to divide the living child in two, and give half to the one and the other half to the other mother. The real mother cried 'O my lord, give her the living child, and in no wise slay it.' The other said 'let it be neither mine nor thine; divide it.' If she could not have a child, the other one should not have one, either.

This is the power of envy, never as vulgar in public as in private, which, adjusted to current requirements, to the ends and the means of the market economy and its values, has become the foundation on which the existing social order, and also disorder, rests. It is also the source of so many tragedies. Impotent and dissatisfied, the individual can easily let his Platonic hatred turn into open hostility towards the world; and on a rainy Sunday afternoon, lost somewhere between the delights of virtual reality and the Towers of St. Pancras station and with nothing much to do, he or she can viciously turn into a vandal. 'In a velvet coffin, my destiny now carries me on its shoulders', Nikiphoros Vrettakos, the Greek Christian-Marxist poet, melancholically propounded.

In the same way, defined, not by what we are or would like to be, but by what we are denied, the syndromes of our negativity and the destructive impulses our presumed exclusion has on our psyche – depression, persecution and vindictiveness – we strive proudly to ascertain our rights. These rights, in their civilised form, are transformed into demands for equality and social justice denied to us by that very system which articulates them as rights. Ineluctably they are then translated into one language only, that of financial claims for help towards our centrally heated existence.

Claims, just as the law which in its majestic impartiality punishes indiscriminately both the poor and the rich caught stealing bread, are not always all that convincing or as morally upright as they purport to be. This does not, of course, imply that people should not demand a fair share of the national wealth, whose increase, incidentally, rather than remove the relative poverty of individuals, has impoverished them further for the actual material demands on life have increased more in proportion. Nor does it mean that discomfort is preferable to the comfort money can buy – I would rather be unhappy in a taxi than at the bus stop waiting in the rain in vain for the bus to come. People need to enjoy their fair share – Justice in the distribution of the national wealth, though 'in accordance with merit in some sense', Aristotle said, is a must in a democracy.

But claims far above what decency demands are as disagreeable as a ketchup stain on the claimant's tie. Pay claims of the latter kind, if and when made, reflect the free market's way of thinking, underpin its priorities and structure of needs and often help to sustain the asymmetries and imbalances they intend to extirpate. Further, they fuel resentment, frustration, consumerism and discontent, the perpetuation of social and professional hierarchies and the stratification of society. They can, indeed, be the absolute denial of equality in whose realm we are supposed to live.

Claiming more is, indeed, self-defeating when it simply glorifies the capitalist logic of needs designed with the precise purpose of denying their satisfaction, and when aspirations, transformed into entitlements, contribute to the rise of unfulfilled expectations which leave the individual permanently dissatisfied. The man of boundless desires, Socrates said, is like a leaky jar – never filled, never satisfied. The degradation of life, the violation of what Raymond Williams called 'essential equality', is the inevitable result, reinforced, as French sociologist Pierre Bourdieu established, by education which, rather than eliminate differences only endorses pre-existent social distinctions. For Williams, 'essential equality' demands that everybody is treated with the respect due to a human being regardless of his or her condition or position. His ideal was, of course, dismissed as ludicrous like all those that, as Orwell caustically remarked, only an intellectual could entertain.

The same one-dimensional needs in a society defined by them are even more powerfully projected when they are translated as consumer rights. Associations articulate the need of the consumers to be protected against all odds, including their own crassitude, and relatives of people lost in tragedies find consolation in monetary compensation, hopefully as large as possible. Hospital patients need to be compensated for the mistakes of the medical profession, and social workers translate their clients' needs into financial claims. Happiness, understood as a life of blissful unconcern in a Constable painting, has become a need with a 'hedonistic' value attached to it. Failing to get it, we have to find someone to blame in order to extract payment, the compensation we deserve for the lost blessedness we are entitled to. Though often meritless, frivolous and purely mercenary, utterly distasteful when pursued on the grounds that there is no accident which is not someone else's fault, such claims are, however, somehow necessary to pursue.

But rights of this kind are founded on the same distorted cultural assumptions, the same polluted perceptions that define only materially our needs and our 'rights' to a perfect life. They give us a group identity that has nothing to do with our basic human needs and reduce everything to a monetary affair. Transformed from human beings into consumers proud to have rights, consumer rights, which, as opposed to those of human beings, have to be, and are, scrupulously observed, is not a cause for self-congratulation. It sounds more like an absurdity flying blindly at the bottom of the black hole of an abiotic mode of existence.

Desire, French novelist Marcel Proust held, is a tireless 'transformational machine'. It transforms us, but it cannot take us where we want to go. We try, as poet Rainer Maria Rilke put it, to 'conquer littleness, obtaining success that only makes us small, while, unconstrained and unconstraining, the permanent eludes us all'.

Besides, we cannot arrive because there is no arrival point. Trying to make the impossible dream come true, we end up working harder to pay off the debt for the Renault we bought two years ago, which is outdated now, and the high mortgage for that beautiful home we never see because we have to work so hard to keep up with payments. Banking on our insatiable desire for more and better, helping us but not helpfully enough, capitalism gives in so many ways less and worse. We head for its open arms only to fall into its hands. The illusion that this is what life is about is necessary because without it there is only nothingness, and not all that much of it. Occasionally we need, of course, to cry out to show we are not dead.

As Anacharsis, the poet, put it, the first cup is for thirst, the second for pleasure, the third for intemperance and the rest for madness. It seems that we, in our digital wisdom, cannot tell the difference.

3. The Royal Road to Somebodiness

Image, and its immoderately priced illusions, is the obsession of the age, the panacea to the dark anonymity of life, the royal road to somebodiness. The image, Umberto Eco's 'epidermic self-awareness', though virtual and unauthentic, a digital replica created for special effects, is a verity we can no longer separate from its simulated projection. It overshadows the undeclared reality and becomes reality itself, the terrain on which any woman who knows her Bridget Jones will meet all her future husbands.

This is what the illusions corporation banks on. It invites us to make our statements by the way we present, entertain or take care of ourselves, the way we furnish our home, eat or holiday. In the commodities world, no item is desirable because of its use value. The only thing of importance is the image it represents, the illusion it creates, the style denoting the latest in thinking which we had better adopt if we want to look gorgeous, successful and desired, celebrities in front of our mirror, men good enough for women to pardon, as Saki, the Scottish writer put it, 'a generous measure of mental deficiency'. The market, in whose pragmatism we swim, tells us everything we need to know on the subject.

The marketing of ourselves as much as of cereal or of the slaughtering of those who, prime minister Tony Blair said, 'have no compunction about killing the innocent', rests on packaging and image involving emotional engagement. Real men smoke Marlboro cigarettes, gorgeous men use Gillette razor blades, adventurous men drive Range Rovers. Likewise, sensual women love Cadbury's chocolates, 'classy' women use L'Oreal creams which combat cellulite and wrinkles – a claim which L'Oreal failed to back up when questioned by the British Advertising Standards Authority – wholesome women use Persil washing powder. Commodities, Raymond Williams observed, are never good enough in themselves:'they must be validated, if only in fantasy, by association with social and personal meanings.'

Meanings do of course change according to the times. In 1961, Buick sold its cars by telling 'you' that driving one 'unmistakably tells your success'. A few years later, in 1966, Volkswagen, banking on consumer disgust with the consumer society, became 'real', 'honest', 'down to earth': 'If you want to show you've gotten somewhere', its witty revolutionary ad read, 'get a beautiful chariot. But if you simply want to get somewhere, get a bug.'

Ever since, the advertising industry has embraced the counter-culture, those unmentionable public fears of conformity, manipulation, artificiality, phoniness, fraud or powerlessness. It harnesses, as Thomas Frank in his *The Conquest of Cool* says, public mistrust of consumerism to the cause of consumerism itself. 'Thanks to BP, lobster is back on the menu at the Tate', the BP ad read under a 1738 Charles Collins' painting of a lobster on a Delft dish. It then pointedly attached to the painting a social message for the very purpose of denying it: 'perhaps', the text read, 'Collins was making a moral point about over-consumption.' The society of consumption is also the society of the denunciation of consumption in the same way mass society is shaped by its denunciation.

Hence the consumer revolt against mass society is often carried out by the counter-culture in the name of individuality – the product pitch is 'Buy This to Escape Consumerism' – or in the name of authenticity, the real thing which is nevertheless as 'classic', 'natural' and 'pure' as its promoters thinking. 'It's the real thing', Coca-Cola's great slogan read before the advertisers decided that the drink can also give you 'real life, real friends and real family'. The latest breed of the same thinking has produced what is called responsible brand association which links superficially healthy eating with its exact opposite, McDonald's hamburgers in this instance. One may well expect, if the trend catches on, Durex to follow suit by endorsing abstinence, Stella Artois by promoting temperance, and Ford extolling the virtues of walking to work. That is how we leave behind the phoniness and the dangers of modern living to return to the cherished old values, the time of innocence, domestic idyll, caramelised apples and candy floss. Saatchi has even dropped the word 'advertising'. 'Ideas', we are told, 'are the currency of the future.'

Personifying 'young thinking', the image represents the 'Now Generation' which implies absolute up-to-dateness. The latter turns youth into a state of mind, instant gratification into the heart's desire, and a craving for the new, even if it embraces food intolerance, into the obsession of our up-to-date unconscious.

Its invitation is often couched in absurd, senseless terms, deliberately shocking like a Houellebecq novel. After all, no TV stars in low-cut gowns inviting us to 'come to bed' on a reclining seat of Virgin Atlantic's Upper class service can fill the drained energy tanks; and no washing powder makes us sexually irresistible or promotes a harmonious family life. Likewise, no women with open, photogenic legs, looking expectantly from London buses towards viewers in the cars behind, 'give a purpose to the brand', in this instance the products of Folke, the clothing company. Glorification of sexual violence as in the ads of Dolce & Gabbana, the Italian fashion company, or pornography, the other trend in advertising that is masquerading as social conscience, Benetton's 'United Colours' is there just to grab our attention. Reality is 'never of much use out here', as in Annie Proulx's *Wyoming Stories*.

But the advertising industry, realising, like all other industries including that of politics, how poorly furnished we are and exploiting consumer fantasies, has long ago rejected the representational logic, the realism of modernism. Its capricious simulation of truth underlines the decline of the referentials that goes hand in hand with the increase in the manipulation of the recipients of its messages.

The deceitful promise the commodity culture makes is that the satisfaction of the needs it can meet will turn us into masters of our individual universe. In reality it turns us into victims of 'the sparkling armada of promises', its manufactured illusions.

Illusion, a product sold in quantities which, though vast, can never meet demand, replaces reality itself. Or, more accurately, reality is recreated through the illusory character of the commodity or, as Jean Baudrillard, the French postmodernist philosopher, said, through a code, such as the digital code, which, real rather than illusory, both enables reality and also bypasses it by breaking the difference between copy and original. His principle of reversibility that made at first his theory seem absurd and far-fetched implies that even death does not really occur.

'Content', detached from 'form', becomes as Wolfgang Fritz Haug, the German Marxist philosopher, said, 'completely disembodied'. The process is facilitated by the inward projection of the image which is necessary if we are to sustain it psychologically in order to nurture our comforting self-deceptions and launch ourselves into the strawberry fields of self-satisfaction. The identification with the image becomes, D.H. Lawrence, the English novelist, said, an instinctive reaction. The pressure comes not only from without, but also from within, from our own uncertainties and low self-esteem, the stream of unfulfilled wishes, the need to escape a reality which, sometimes, screams like a hare caught in a gin. After all, nobody is obsessed with reality – illusions are inevitable, for, as T.S. Eliot, a major figure in English literature since the early 1920s, said, 'humankind cannot bear very much reality.'

At the most elementary level, to conceal a disagreeable reality, in effect to distort it if necessary, we do go, as a rule, to almost any length. We all receive dental treatment, not just to prevent but also to conceal the natural decay of teeth, we wear exquisite clothes to look good but also to disguise body 'imperfections', we smile – those premeditated, ineluctable Blairite smiles, so polished you could shave your face in their reflection – just because we need to look and sound pleasant and self-assured. Looking, sounding or smelling good meets an aesthetic personal need, readily excused for such small and innocuous deceptions. A source of gratification in themselves, they also give us this little extra self-assurance and self-confidence that can make a big difference in our lives.

But often, only too often, to accommodate, conform, please or just survive we choose to forego some of our most essential features. We try to be what we are not, to live, instead of our own life, the life of someone else, that of the person we impersonate, the life of our self-image or the life of our brand constructed by our branding manager and promoted through our personal website. Myshkin, the hero of Dostoevsky's *The Idiot*, tried to be himself, a truly good and honest man in a morally bankrupt society, and ended up as the 'idiot', the word being uttered mercilessly behind his back until his disintegration. Streetwise, instead of meeting our own needs, we rush, thus, to meet the needs of the image we project, that of the man or woman we think we ought to look like, cool with a pair of sunglasses after dark or on the tube, desirable, successful, or the image of a person of authority, responsibility, stillness, nonchalance or whatever else we are under pressure to prove we are in order to earn approval or respect. The man who kept turkeys before he advanced to the more important job of minding the cows has to dress and behave in a way befitting his new rank. Self-presentation, incidentally, just like art, does not reproduce reality; it interprets it, instead, liberally and unfaithfully. At the end the original self may look a poor, embarrassing relation to its carved out copy, but, as in art, all that matters is the image.

But as a result we are no longer ourselves, which we refuse to own, but the image of ourselves which we have allowed others to own for us. This image, inseparable from its rewards, is what will impress the girls at the party, our colleagues and clients, the bank manager, the boss and often our own selves. It is what will enable us to market ourselves as a valuable human commodity twice as ordinary as anybody else, and, therefore, interact with the world in the most profitable way. In the 'Caring Nineties', remote as the time when Madonna was still a virgin, this did, at least, require a caring-looking face. Not any more. Being unprofitable, such a face vanished many a summer ago. What the world respects today are 'winners', and 'winners' we must look even if, for the purpose, we need to employ managers and agents, PR consultants, advertisers and plastic surgeons who will give us a wrinkle-free existence and restore our 'right' to beauty. 'You suddenly realise', the Czech novelist Milan Kundera, seized by amazement, pondered, 'that it's all just one face in many variations and that no such a thing as an individual ever existed.' The 'uniqueness' we project is often engraved on water.

Society, naturally, is not interested in our virtues. Rather than character, substance and wisdom, what we value is personality, looks and information. In a society of zeroes, heroes are not men and women of character but the idols of consumption – pop singers, models, footballers or film stars who impersonate real life heroes. Although their failures or falls from grace make us feel better about ourselves, society does not really want to know, and we do not want society to know, either, about our loneliness and private pains, the uncertainties and the hassles of daily life, the fears and vulnerabilities that undermine the whole of our existence. Hence, hiding in intricate social patterns and their elaborate vagueness, we present ourselves through a mask. If they have not died out, genuine feelings, a whole species of them, go into the safe – on display are only their imitations. Well protected by 'our own artful dodges to escape from the grim shadow of self-knowledge', Joseph Conrad, the Polish-born novelist who learned English after the age of 21 and wrote it like few others, said rather stingingly, we hide even from our own selves.

'Not even our internal monologues', James Joyce reflected, 'are our own.' So infected by a lifestyle sold in magazines, Gerty MacDowell, a character in one of his novels, could not tell whether her feelings were a sincere expression of her own self or of the woman she impersonated to look like the woman she thought she ought to look like. The 'I' ends up a misrepresentation of the true self, and 'I', if one can hide the evidence, is no longer 'I'. What we have is only what we pretend. Caught in the glittering dentures of our synthetic culture, in an alien world that feeds on lack of feeling, indifference, aggression, exploitation, hatred and frustration, we do not know who 'I' is, the one we show the world, the one who we fear it really is, or the confused synthesis of the two. Perhaps, after all, this 'I' does not exist. 'I search myself with my hands', a puzzled Yannis Ritsos, the poet who found himself often at the edge of madness, wrote; '... I'm missing.'

It could, of course, be argued that there is not just one self, identical only with itself, but many, each of whom, constantly remaking itself while trying to assert itself over the others, pulls us in a different direction. It could, therefore, be that it is neither possible nor even desirable to be fully true to ourselves, for some aspects of it, those incompatible with man's actual mode of life, are always sacrificed. This is the assumption on which the psychoanalytic concept of repression rests. There is, therefore, no such a thing as an authentic human nature, an authentic essence of the social, with its needs, its own will, its own values, its finalities. To be more objective, Baudrillard suggested, one would have to acknowledge 'a radical uncertainty as to our own desires, our own choice, our own opinion, our own will', perhaps even our most basic understandings – 'now tell me dad,' my daughter asked me when she was five, 'who is my real au pair?' At least consistent with his views, Baudrillard extended the uncertainty to his own life, preferring to be a man without a background.

Yet nothing seems to matter except the final result: the projection of the best selling image of our always natural selves – that of youth, health, energy, personality, good looks, connections, charm, good taste, sophistication, success. For this we enlist all the help we can get from beauticians, dieticians, masseurs, plastic surgeons, fashion designers, magazine columnists, personal trainers or products – anything that would put us on the fast track on the road to 'success'. 'A whole generation of our best and brightest', Germaine Greer, the Australian writer, lamented, 'is learning the meretricious act of instant appeal, with spending power as the only indicator of personal worth'. You fail to sell yourself as a goldmine, and you feel you are worthless.

Illusions, our virtual reality, sustain our existence, give it meaning and purpose, and a language to interpret the world. To top the cake, they can also give us a girlfriend, one who, though only a programme on a computer, can communicate with us over the internet-capable mobile phone as coquettishly and intimately as a Watteau painting. Cheap as the Sardinian prisoners brought to Rome by Tiberius Gracchus and offered for sale at any price, illusions are, to recall Ludwig Wittgenstein, the Austrian-born analytical philosopher, the most essential feature of 'an age without culture' which is our age. If we could cash them, poverty would be no more.

This illusionary world is our apple of Samarkand, the bubble full of emptiness we live in, the big lie which, if taken away, can leave us homeless. The fear, as the image industry tells us, is that if we do not live up to it, if we do not conceal or distort our most essential features, we will be left behind in the race to 'succeed'. The terrible stress this fear to be who we are creates is one of the problems given by a life built on false premises. The other is the gradual loss of our ability to tell the difference between the real and the illusionary, life and gameshow.

Living at the edge of our being, in the multicoloured confusion beamed into our living rooms by satellite, in a blank ambiguity reminiscent of a Warhol painting, we end up unsure as to which desires are the really important ones, which needs are authentic, which self is the real one to axe or imitate. Trapped in the maze of our reality, we cannot distinguish truth from falsehood, the original from its echo. False creates taste, as Howard Rheingold, the 'professional virtual community builder', remarked; and falsity reinforces itself by eliminating any possible reference to the authentic which is reconstructed to resemble the false. We do not know what we really want or who we really are. The market determines it for us. Even our dreams are doctored, Chacko says in Arundhati Roy's *The God of Small Things*.

Obsessed with this superimposed reality, unable only too often to separate reality itself from its simulated projection, from the illusion that looks back at us and laughs out of the other side of its mouth, we deny in the process our own self, truth and needs and remain as connected to our disintegrating world as the man who did not know anybody. Euripides puts in Helen's mouth the words of a legend: 'It was an image of me. I never went to Troy' to which the messenger responded: 'You mean it was for a phantom, for nothing we did all that work?' The story, mentioned by Stesichorus, the sixth-century BC poet, was that the Goddess Hera had formed an image of Helen out of pure air with which she duped Paris.

Duped like him, deluded by images, encompassed by a cloud almost impenetrable by candour, we go unthinkingly for products to sustain our illusions about who and what we are, we forego living in a way that makes sense to ourselves and try, instead, to live up to an image of which we are victims rather than creators. In the delusive pursuit of self-fulfilment, in the toneless void of an incorporeal existence, the image eventually becomes our inner self, which, as empty as a discarded can of beer, echoes and re-echoes the splendour of our failures. 'Solitude was the climate in (our) head, emptiness was the partner in (our) bed, pain echoed in the steps of (our) tread', Maya Angelou, the black American playwright and poet, ruefully concluded.

The cost of all this is, indeed, too heavy. We are, however, willing to bear it if the price looks right.

4. Everyone But an Idiot

Life is physically easier nowadays. But we cannot take advantage of it because we have to work hard to earn enough to buy what is socially validated as good. Convinced that we have to meet the needs society tells us we must in order to make life worth living, we give away what makes life worth living. Rather than play with, and enjoy, our children, we work hard to buy for them the toys which will colour their disconnections. Rather than spend time with the wife, we labour to earn the money to pay the solicitor's fees for the divorce settlement. Rather than enjoy the company of friends, we slave to earn enough to buy a new car good enough to impress all those friends we do not see. Of value is considered to be only what has a price-tag attached to it. What has no price has no value.

Unable to strike the right balance between work and life, in bed with a laptop rather than a human being, without emotional nourishment, and often short of sleep and, therefore, irritable, we end up burning the candle at both ends. The challenge posed is nearly impossible to meet. The sea has turned into yogurt, historian Tasos Vournas, an elderly friend of mine used to say during the sexual revolution of the 1960s, but we no longer have spoons. To earn their living, the cows have to die.

To satisfy our needs – intellectual, physical, emotional and spiritual – we need freedom from necessity and mundane considerations. This is the freedom the poor do not have and hence, as Plato said, they are not masters of themselves. Life is, indeed, enjoyable only beyond the struggle of existence; the non-repressive order is essentially an order of abundance. Oscar Wilde's Lady Bracknell did not fail to notice it when she graciously referred to 'the influence of a permanent income on thought'.

But it is here that we find ourselves trapped, for the more we try to master necessity by turning everything into a means to this end the less free we become. On the sclerotic ground of daily realities, we end up consuming ourselves in the struggle to gain freedom from necessity, forgetting in the process the purpose of the exercise and becoming unconsciously the servants of a system that supposedly serves us. In effect, we are trading our freedom for the material rewards we seek as the means to win our freedom. We do everything to gain control over our destiny only to lose it in the process. Rather than give us what it promises, commodified labour just devalues life.

Hence, when it was introduced, labour was resisted. Freed from feudal servitude and oppression and with no means of survival other than selling their labour, people did not see the inhumane, immoderate, alienated daily labour as a gift. They opposed the commodification of their existence and fought against their proletarianization. 'Free' labour was eventually and rather brutally forced upon them by the law. Persons refusing to work and living idly for three days, England decreed in 1547, 'should be branded with a red-hot iron on the breast with the letter V, and should be adjudged the slave for two years, of any person who should inform against such idler.' There were further and much heavier penalties for those attempting to escape their predicament. A person who attempted to escape his temporary enslavement would be made a slave for life, and anyone guilty of a second attempt to escape 'shall have judgment to suffer pains and execution of death as a felon and as enemies of the Commonwealth'. People were left with no choice but, to quote Jonathan Swift, the eighteenth century Irish satirist, work or serve the King.

Like war, labour has nevertheless won respectability. Reputed for its immortality, it is even revered. Adam Smith, just like John Locke a century earlier, saw in it the source of all wealth never seen, however, by all those who, César Vallejo, the poet and one of the founders of the Peruvian socialist party, said, had 'to walk all the way from Trujillo to Lima to earn a wage less than money'; and Marx considered it to be the source of all productivity. Incidentally, Marx, 'congenitally unsuited for any regular employment' according to his biographer Francis Wheen, attempted only twice to be gainfully employed during his thirty-four years in London. David Hume argued that work is, perhaps just like smoking, what differentiates humans from the animals; and New Ager Matthew Fox saw work as 'a gift from God'. Fully unaware of the nuanced sense of the absurd inherent in his statement, the Catholic ex-clergyman added that work is 'a joy, a pleasure, a celebration, even an enchantment'. Opening the doors for the rich at Claridge's puts one, apparently, on the road to the vestibules of paradise. 'Things thought too long can be no longer thought', Yeats would have said.

Nowadays, without fear of being molested by the state if we choose to live idly, we sell, instead, our labour to the highest bidder available. If we could, nevertheless, have what we wanted without having to give our time and energy to someone else, in all probability, we would not work, or, at least, we would not work if 'the pleasure in the work itself', as William Morris, the Victorian socialist, argued, was not there. As Arthur Young, an eighteenth century writer, said candidly: 'Everyone but an idiot knows that the lower classes must be kept poor ... or they will not work.' The result is alienation from work, alienation from what is, unfortunately, in the very centre of our lives, the silent screams of our unimplemented purpose.

Knackered by the day's hard work, pursued by the clock, the loathsome advance of numbers, individuals have neither the time nor the strength to read a book, shop and cook or enjoy the pleasures of sex. Sex is the last thing in mind at the end of a long day at the office, the ensuing struggle to get on the bus home and then the management of the takeaway Chinese leftovers from yesterday's meal. Nor can they invite friends for dinner, a pleasure, which as shepherd Eumaios told Odysseus, is given by the Gods when they want to be nice to humans, parent their children or participate in the shaping of their communities, what Edmund Burke, the British eighteenth century political writer, called the 'little platoons'. Burke, incidentally, did not mean by this useful term autonomous social units, but groups in which people know their particular rank in the social hierarchy, which is part of a natural, God-given order.

Life is constantly harassed and agitated, stretching the individuals and their families to breaking point. Saving time turns, under these circumstances, into a major exercise carried out with the use of big freezers to store frozen chickens grown on hormones and antidepressants, microwaves to cook them, cars to move around fast and domestic help to manage home and children. For all this, one has of course to work longer hours, being made in turn even more dependent on paid help and machines.

Technology's bewildering, breakneck pace, dictated by corporate executives, genetically modified but still human enough to need a hug or two in any fiscal year, cannot offer emancipation from necessity. Rather than liberate, technology has enslaved, and rather than expand time, it has compressed it even more. Its innovations, always heralded as gifts to mankind, are immediately used to meet other needs created by the innovations themselves. Forcing us to keep learning, not in order to improve ourselves, but just survive, it eats further into our time, and increases stress levels. The information explosion – millions of internet sites, CD-Roms, multipurpose mobile phones and hundreds of TV channels – makes the effort just to access, much less absorb, news and views a twitching agony when already just reading the Sunday newspaper has become an almost Herculean task. Ostensibly at the service of humans, technology has reduced Being, Martin Heidegger, the German philosopher, said, to its functionalism – hence his dismissal of technology as the last flagpole of metaphysics or humanism.

Ironically, there was a period, in the 1960s, the time a man's politics could be safely guessed from his beard, that we thought otherwise. The emerging technological revolution was full of promises – 'undreamed-of living standards and the possibility of leisure on an unbelievable scale', as British prime minister Harold Wilson, perhaps sincerely, chose to put it. The same period also gave us a headache – how best to spend the huge chunks of work-free time.

Technological advances and a client-driven culture, giving voice to the night, have further encouraged many people to work at all hours – check the voice-mail before going to bed, email at midnight and receive a reply immediately, or type away on a laptop in the middle of a sunny beach or a café. Unprofitable moments are lifeless shadows of what has been and is no longer – just like smoking in the presence of ladies. Owing also to other factors such as outsourcing, downsizing or psychological insecurities that force employees to be available all the time or create workaholic tendencies, the pressure becomes almost irresistible. The number of people working more than sixty hours a week rose to one in six from one in eight. Working all hours has become the norm – the nine to five job is becoming as extinct as the habit of sending handwritten letters. 'Time famine', the current term used to describe the stress under which we live, means only one thing: that we have lost control of our lives. Even if unemployed or retired, one is still 'hurry sick', unable to find the time even to read. Life is longer, time is shorter.

'People hurry,' Yannis Ritsos, the poet, wondered in Athens in amazement. 'They are in a hurry to go away, to get away (from what?), to get (where?) – I don't know ... In these streets, another time they had passed with huge flags, they had a voice (I remember, I heard it), an audible voice. Now they walk, they run, they hurry, motionless in their hurry.' Although we do much more in a day than we ever did, there is more to do than ever. Time, the father of our days, has shrunk; and so have relations, the mother of our lives. The milk train doesn't stop here anymore.

Yet in spite of all our efforts, a lifetime committed to work, in spite also of the fact that now it takes two incomes to achieve the minimum living standard, sometimes we cannot buy even basic security. No matter how hard we work to flesh the dream, the latter, like a Soviet five-year plan, remains a dream, the insomniac's dream clothed with our desires and declothed by our limitations. Beneath the periodic euphoria of the stock market, sampled by the top one per cent of the population who own half of all shares, the promises of the dotcoms and rising house prices, there is private unease and stress. General job uncertainty involving the threat of unemployment, poverty and even destitution, is suspended over the heads of the middle class, too, with the demise of jobs-for-life expectations and the arrival of what Charles Handy, the management guru, called 'portfolio lives', i.e. careers spanning multiple activities and employers, if indeed we have employers at all. Temporary or part-time work are distinct possibilities; and no one can be certain of a decent pension – hence people choose these days to work even beyond retirement age.

Work is not necessarily unpleasant or unrewarding in non-monetary terms. One can well be pleased with the status or the identity the job confers upon the individual, for, as many think, you are what you do, or with the job title, often trivial, that is attached to it. One may be pleased, too, with the job's structure and predictability, its stimulating environment and the social interaction, the responsibility given, the pride one can take in a good performance, or the self-respect one draws from being needed and dependable. A job may equally well give someone something to do and together with it a sense of power missing in all other aspects of his or her life – 'I simply cannot live without power and tyranny over someone else', Fyodor Dostoevsky's Underground Man confessed. It may offer a person, whose personal life is in ruins, the fugitive from life, an escape from reality or provide the safety of daily labour even if all this entails is watching the grass grow. Melisanthe in such a case lets her hair down over the balcony and Pelleas happily climbs up.

Fulfilling work, i.e. the work which fuses with the self, requires, however, more than that. Its value is not in the product or the service itself but in the human being's self-realisation. As 'man's act of self-creation', it has to provide the means by which we can express our creativity, imagination, personal commitment and individuality. Vivaldi, who composed about five hundred concertos, or myself who, like all primitives, can never draw a line between work and leisure, would readily testify to this effect. Work needs to enhance life rather than be a struggle for the provision of the bare essentials, to give us a sense of purpose in line with some sort of a universal purpose, and to be in tune with human rather than market values. The ethical dimension of work to which we are committed as human beings rather than professionals, highlighted by American social scientist Thorstein Veblen, is the alternative to the consumerist ethos of capitalism. This kind of work, which like everything else decisive, comes about, as Nietzsche said, 'in spite of', is nevertheless the property of the privileged few, those who can feel miserable only because they do not have their fair share of misery.

The rest, all presumed peerless individuals free to find bliss in ale and able to outlive their distortions of themselves, objectified, reified, merge in the function of their daily task, spiritually and emotionally unfulfilled. A staggeringly small percentage of people, just five per cent, a survey among 17,000 executives revealed, settle for positions that just pay the bills. Reduced in 'the prosaic severity of the daily task that gives bread' to an abstract and functional identity which fits the requirements of the 'job', they end up as mere replaceable cogs in a wheel. They know it as they know that this is what is expected of them. 'Why should I get a person', Henry Ford, the American motor manufacturer, argued, 'when what I want is a pair of hands?'

Forced by necessity, real or perceived, to do what they would not freely choose to do, they are, thus, degraded into a commodity, separated from both their own selves and each other by the function they perform, self-alienated as Marx famously pronounced in the nineteenth century, when alienation was a synonym for insanity. They live a fraction of their being. The General, in the story of Eugène Ionesco, the Romanian-born playwright, so morally deformed, thought of himself as nothing but a General and used to go to bed in uniform.

Necessary, alienated labour, a human standing-reserve appreciated only in terms of its exchange value is a system of essentially inhuman, mechanical and routine activities. Their pursuit is not designed to enhance individuality and gives no real pleasure. 'Most of what office workers do is pointless or downright wicked', French writer Corinne Maier pointed out after she described salaried work as 'the new slavery'. Hence Freud saw labour as an unpleasantness and Foucault described it as a curse. Kavafis, the undisputed founder of modern Greek poetry, having spent most of his life working in the Department of Irrigation of the Ministry of Public Works until his retirement in 1922, knew something about it;

and so did Kafka who worked with an insurance company. Alienated labour has nothing to do with primary instinctual gratification, for it does not relate to the individual's aptitudes and needs. 'To link', Marcuse stressed, 'performance on the assembly line, in offices and shops with instinctual needs is to glorify dehumanisation as pleasure.' This is, I assume, the reason the Greek heteronymous word for 'work', *douleiá*, is spelt exactly the same as the word 'slavery', *douleía*; only the accent changes.

Under such circumstances, money earned for work done just for the money it pays cannot be greeted with a burst of gratitude, silent or otherwise, for it offers no adequate compensation. Even bonuses and performance pay schemes increase dissatisfaction, for their price is stress, anxiety and depression produced in high-pressure environments; even climbing up the ladder of the hierarchy does not offer adequate rewards as the individuals remain slaves of their function. The task to be performed takes priority over their own interests, as does the time given to earning money as opposed to living a good life. The profit principle is unprofitable to most, and rather disagreeable to all those who have come to earth expecting it to be a better place.

Happiness in work forced upon us remains, therefore, beyond the shores of sober probability. And we know it because our mind, though it has falsified the world's essence, has not done so completely – we still get a flickering reflection of it. Hence few people would choose to give up control over their time, particularly if they have to work at night – the night, Homer said, 'tames both Gods and humans', but that was long before we tamed it. Few would also choose to lose control over the nature, purpose and outcome of the work they do or the use of its products, if the monetary compensation was not their overriding concern. And only a few would describe serving customers at a restaurant, ceaselessly entering figures into a computer or assembling gear boxes on the shop floor as one's life purpose.

This kind of work, 'the tyranny of the unimaginative', does not help the individual to grow, has lost its human meaning and is by definition void of substance. Inept and insensitive to the thrill of the marvel inherent in the flight of the imagination, it is done only for the money it pays. Hence the self-dissatisfaction, the mass production of distraction, the clinical depression and chronic anxiety disorders that affect one in six adults in the UK, the epidemic of stress-related illness on account of which one million British are drawing incapacity benefits instead of working to earn a living. 'Today's world of work', a recent survey from the British Economic and Social Research Council revealed, 'is much less satisfying to employees than the one they were experiencing ten years ago.' Hence also the 'significant deterioration' in employees' commitment to their companies, the increased absenteeism and the lower productivity.

Division of labour, heralded by Adam Smith as the means that will enable us to 'grow rich', only underlines the unpleasantness involved. It limits work, whose intensity has increased as much as the hours of work demanded, to a narrow field in a way which helps the system to become more efficient at the individual's expense. In fact, work has enslaved us in the very name of freedom. We can depend on it for our fulfilment as much as one can depend on a clock stuck at 7.30.

Frustrated and helpless, all we can then do is redouble our efforts to achieve what we no longer remember. The cancelled promises have been obliterated from memory, or perhaps, implicated in unamiable activities, we just do not want to remember, as we know that for most of us there is no escape from work. Work is 'not an ill for mending'. Or, again, we may not even want to escape, for an escape could well be an escape into the land of misery, perhaps, in an empty and cold room that looks, as Costas Taktsis, the Greek novelist who was tragically killed in 1988, would say, like a 'sepulchre where they keep the disentombed bones of the dead'.

Unemployment is not, of course, preferable to work. Of this I have personal and rather bitter experience from the mid-seventies, when unemployed, disillusioned and demoralised, I looked like a casualty of the First Galactic War. Feeling so infinitesimal that nobody would bother even to disapprove of me, an invisible apparition existing perhaps only in my own imagination, all I then wanted was the slavery of work, any work, which would enable me to earn a living and together with it my dignity and self-respect; and I could not have it. The impact was devastating, the pain excruciating, the self-pity overwhelming. A man of tremendous impotence swiftly fulfilling his potentials, I had, or so it looked, to postpone living for another time. Some do, of course, claim that, by virtue of its being beyond economic rationality and external constraint, unemployment can be a potentially emancipatory process. If this is so, I just missed it.

The non-biodegradable Victorian rhetoric focusing on hard work, thrift, self-reliance, respect for the law, devotion to the family and charity – the values one might call the moral economy – has not given the individual what it promised. Life beyond the realm of necessity receives no institutional support. It is outside the flow of money, beyond the grasp of a language incapable of entertaining volatile concepts or elusive ideas not amenable to measurement. Values, E.P. Thompson, the British social historian, argued, are not 'imponderables'. The system's intellectual police made sure, of course, that his views were dismissed as insubstantial and vaporous; substantial and solid for it is only money, the 'ambrosial cash' as Byron called it, which can buy life at a discount. Death costs even less. 'Why live', a sign, seen by Sigmund Freud in an American cemetery, asked its customers, perhaps more than rhetorically, 'when you can be buried for ten dollars?'

The excellent bridge to happiness that materialism has built is rather too short. We cross it only to find ourselves, not on the other side, but in the middle of nowhere, in the heart of a motley illusion, empowering as befuddlement and fulfilling as an absence.

However, though shocked as if we had just heard that Babylon had fallen, and yet anything but surprised, we can console ourselves that this absence is all our own.

5. Anything Goes

Travelling, as George Seferis, the poet, says, 'among yellow trees in driving rain', alone in an alienated and alienating world, we are our sole point of reference, the sum total of everything there is, the world's inner essence. As Schopenhauer, the 19th century German philosopher, insisted to the applause of some of our contemporaries, we contain everything, including the most distant galaxies, within ourselves. Conversely, the world seems to contain nothing but our 'I', complete as the lost arms of Aphrodite of Milos. Hence our reality is the reality, and our truth is the truth. Reality and truth, internalised like a rebuff and personalised like car number plates, are our property. True is what is true for you, good is what is good for you, beautiful is what is beautiful for you. Truth is in the eye of the beholder, and judgment a matter of personal preference or taste.

The rule, articulated in the universities of lost causes in the depressing '70s and the esurient '80s, is that there are no eternal and universal truths to be guided by, no principles to adhere to. General world views, metanarratives and ideologies, certainties and absolutes which in the name of freedom, civilisation, 'our' nation, religion or socialism repressed or exterminated millions of people, Jean-François Lyotard, the French postmodernist philosopher, argued, provide merely a 'credible' reason for action in the interests of what legitimises power. Carrying on in the same philosophical tradition, initially established by Protagoras, who had denied objective truth in virtue, and Gorgias, who maintained that nothing exists, and, if it does, it is unknowable, and, if it is knowable to one, it cannot be communicated to others, Foucault, too, dismissed the usefulness of general world views, the metanarratives and their 'fuzzy and porous' concepts whether Christian, liberal or Marxist. Each society, he argued, has its own regime of truth, its general politics of truth, shaped by language and enveloped into an ideology.

Michel Foucault, together with Jacques Derrida, questioned the western search for truth – the prime western illusion – and objected to immortal verities, the eviternal self-deception into which we are pushed by grand designs only to feel betrayed at the end and ready, after a pause, to jump again into another comforting self-deception.

The revolt against all absolute and universal truths, those decreed by an omnipresent cosmic mother-in-law, was successfully completed by the end of the millennium, and the crystals of the pompous old certainties were shattered. Truth, objective truth, the metaphysics of modernity, gave up the ghost like a fish, belly up; and its various violent lovers lost their virility. Looking for absolute truths looked like searching for the Loch Ness monster or Iraqi Weapons of Mass Destruction.

As a result, we no longer felt obliged to abide by the commands of any authority, spiritual or secular, and we do not have to conform to any authorised version of 'eternal' requirements. We do not likewise defer to our 'betters' because there are no 'betters', and we are 'non-judgmental' because anything is as good as anything else. Qualities, once believed to be as hard as rock, have been transformed by relativism into liquid truths taking the shape of their containers and virtue has become personal, as personal as our silences. Remodelled by a scepticism awed by that excessive respect with which it is being treated by itself, the concept of a virtuous life is vague and amorphous. The boundaries between right and wrong, good and bad, objective and subjective, drawn in the mist of our uncertainties, are blurred. Nobody can tell us 'objectively' what 'freedom', 'beauty', 'merit', 'knowledge' and 'progress' mean.

The opposites have collapsed, or they have become interchangeable. Everything is undecidable – beauty and ugliness, Left and Right, true and false, useful and useless, real and imaginary. Rome does not need a Cato – Carthage has gone, 'the opposite shore has vanished', and, as Greek surrealist poet and painter Nicos Engonopoulos suggested, 'you might say it never existed'.

Committed, as we are, to liberation from intolerable universalisms, living in the cracks of life beyond good or bad, we cannot set ethical standards because we do not look forward to standards. The world, cynical as the mattress of a downtown hotel room, has no shared concerns, values or aims, no sense of common purpose. So possessed by individual rights, Amitai Etzioni, the US sociologist, and fellow academics such as William Galston and Mary Ann Glendon said, we have even lost sight of our obligations towards each other. The whole no longer exists. 'On this shore,' as Yannis Ritsos conceded, 'we – short-sighted, harassed, and much preoccupied – cannot see it at all, can't even imagine it, by no means can imagine it.' Morally and intellectually indifferent to anything but ourselves, we do not care about anything but ourselves. Of course, things sometimes look dreadful. But 'so what?', 'Who cares?', Quentin Tarantino, the postmodernist Hollywood director, going beyond all ethical questions, asks.

Hence the postmodernist non-judgmental, ophidian attitude, the 'contextualism' which regards the validity of norms only within their own context. Hence also the system theorists' dismissal of the possibility of justifying anything by reference to common principles – societies, we are told, are too complex for the purpose. The individual, Niklas Luhmann, the German sociologist and metaphysician asserted, cannot even find something common to all humanity, which means that Kantian universality becomes a repressive ideological pursuit. Even if we wanted to remain true to something, we do not know what that 'something' is, for we cannot answer the question whose values, ethical or moral, we should adhere to. In the unerring nothingness of satellite television screens or, as Larkin would have it, at 'a time unrecommended by event', the search for standards has been abandoned at the steps of the invisible, unseen and now forgotten.

Free to be whom we want to be without external controls or sentiments of guilt or self-reproach, we can, thus, invest our time and energy in the inhuman pursuit of happiness. Imperatives are no longer. Nobody can really tell us who and what we ought to be. The fear, inhibitions or shame experienced by previous generations are no longer there to torment us – society can tolerate even heterosexuality. Moral pronouncements, analytic philosopher A.J. Ayer said, are 'pure expressions of feeling' as significant as grunts of pain, expressions of our personal approval or disapproval. We live, as a result, through extremeties, author J M Coetzee said, for there has not been a great deal of resistance in any direction.

Subjectivised, privatised like a public utility, truth ended up as nothing more than the pale reflection of a concocted story written posthumously to celebrate life. Its expansive emptiness became the ideology of café lattes, sleek cellphones, vodka and cranberry juice, Tuscan-tiled stainless steel kitchens, whole grains, organic chocolate, concerns about Tibet or other things equally remote, and colourless thoughts as interesting as the suspended passions of soporific echoes. It contains nothing and not all that much of it. In its buffet cynicism helps itself, not with a fork, but with a rake. But we have freedom, the freedom to watch on the small screen the in-filling of Pamela Anderson's vacancies. 'We have independence, General', his men told Simon Bolivar, the hero who pushed the Spanish out of South America. 'So now tell us what to do with it.'

Enveloped in the new culture's ambiguity and indeterminacy, we can no longer describe our world. We would not even accept the possibility of describing it because nothing has any essential qualities on the strength of which a description can be made. Concepts such as 'man', 'Englishness', 'femininity', 'Christianity', 'Marxism', 'civilisation', a 'good life' or 'universal' values that transcend cultural differences have become impossible to determine. To determine them, one would have to establish the core properties, or clusters of properties, which are always present in all and only those things which are described by a common name. But the current anti-essentialist culture tells us that nothing is essential enough to validate a definition.

Jacques Derrida, the 'magus of deconstruction', made the point when he argued against Jean-Jacques Rousseau's thesis according to which nature needs to be listened to because it is identical to itself. Yet, Derrida said, though presumed self-sufficient, sometimes nature cannot provide as, for example, when a mother has no milk for her baby. Nature's nature is, therefore, contradictory, for self-sufficiency and the lack of it cannot both form the basis of its identity, or of what Derrida called its 'self-presence'. Identity is neither pure nor given. Everything is what we understand it to be; and anything is as good as anything else. Of course, when anything is 'good', nothing is good. The centre moves to the periphery, and, as it is no longer, there is no periphery either. With nothing outside our own selves, with meanings deprived of any interiority and things dispossessed of any essence, we cannot even be alienated. You cannot be alienated from what does not exist.

Though likely to be overwhelmed by its own insignificance, anything, being as good as anything else, is equal to anything else. The interests of a stamp-collector, Jean-François Lyotard and Jean Baudrillard asserted, are as important as those of a politician. In the same way, the Romantics of the nineteenth century considered the boyhood of Bathyllus, the beautiful boy of Samos loved by both Polycrates, the tyrant, and Anacreon, the poet, of more moment than the manhood of Napoleon. As interestingly, the British public, polled by the History Channel, viewed Princess Diana's death as more important than both world wars or women winning the vote. In the same spirit of meritless equality, when the unthinkable becomes ordinary, the post-industrial vulgarity of the Los Angeles ghettos, so eagerly brought to our screens by the Hollywood moguls, is as splendid 'in its context' as the 'excellent endowments' of Jane Austen's mind, and a drawing made by the river boatman north of nowhere as much of a masterpiece as Botticelli's Birth of Venus. The United States, though it does not have the history of Europe, can in such circumstances be confidently expected to catch up with her very soon.

What matters is particularity and difference, recognition of the proclaimed value only within its own specific context; and context-specific truth-claims cannot be assessed on the strength of larger evaluative or interpretative criteria but only in terms of their own meanings and values. They are discourse dependent. Consequently, we are not in a position to judge what is outside our own cultural perimeter, in George Seferis' verse, 'unknown tongues of Babel without relation to the grammar, to the Lives of the Saints or the Book of Psalms'. Nothing exists outside its own context. In the church of relativism where the best jokes for a funeral – that of moral, ethical and aesthetic values – can be heard, important is the contingent rather than the universal, the subjective rather than the objective, the specific rather than the general, the parts rather than the whole. The relativisation of meaning, Panajotis Kondylis, the Greek philosopher who lived between Heidelberg and Athens and died in 1998 at the early age of 55, said, is only the latest strategy for advancing social equality and evacuating non-democratic opinions associated with an elitist past.

It follows that in the absence of universal truths, we have no right to project our own values onto the whole world, for they are neither better nor worse than those of the Others. They just are. Giving equal space to all cultures, the American Liberal Association described Shakespeare, Goethe and James Joyce as 'dead white European males', and trying to find a reason for ethnic pupils' poor performance at school, teachers asserted that those pupils' culture has 'a different way of knowing'. Rational discussion in this or other similar contexts, precluded by the guilt generated by the previous total rejection of other cultures, is viewed as an attempt to repress non-literate forms of expression.

The facts-based western search for truth, the rationalism on which our civilisation is founded, is rejected on the same grounds. Reason is just as good as intuition and beliefs, and science just one more belief system. The 9,400-year-old Spirit Cave Man found in North America and the 9,300-year-old Kennewick Man found in Washington State both have Caucasoid features suggesting they are of European or Middle Eastern descent. This indicates that the peopling of America is more complex than it was thought and that the Native American needs to be redefined. Yet for postmodernist anthropology, whatever explanation science may give after extracting DNA from those skeletons is good but no better than the mystical beliefs of the Native Americans themselves about their prehistory. Science is just one of many ways of knowing the world, just as valid as shamanic myth. Likewise, Darwin's 'satanic' theory of evolution, as the American religious fundamentalists claim, is another 'origins myth' to be discounted despite all the evidence from the fossil record, geobiology and molecular biology. We cannot tell one thing from another.

The whole, having surrendered to the philosophy, ideology and politics of fragmentation, disfigured, is nothing more than an abstract legal entity without any cultural underpinning – historical, ethical, social, political or even linguistic. Hence respect for Otherness, which turned into identity politics, what Raymond Williams, a member of a working-class family, called 'militant particularism', turned decisively against the whole. Instead of the old concerns, prominence was given, instead, to issues relating to the groups' social status, the right to be different and proud of it. Immigrant communities rejected integration and demanded what was called 'differentiated citizenship' that involved state recognition of their religious holidays, exemption from laws that interfere with their religious affairs, protection of their conventions, customs and family practices or state funding for the teaching of mother-tongue languages. As political philosopher Joseph Raz put it, the ability of ethnic minorities to choose is intimately tied up with both access to their culture and the respect accorded to it by the majority.

Society for this kind of politics, which with the new millennium lost its lustre, exists only in its constituent parts, subgroups or 'communities' with their own leaders which the body politic, reconstituted, needs to recognise. The system, the whole, the totality are presumed non-existent and, naturally, what is not existent can neither be challenged nor, much less, transformed. 'Political correctness', the self-appointed thought police ever ready to turn nasty at very short notice, made sure that deviations would not be tolerated. Women may not be called women any longer, but 'womyn'.

Islamism, having turned into an ideology calling for the dissolution of social and cultural formations, added one more dimension to the ongoing fragmentation, the religious, which goes hand in hand with the racial. The new black man in America, Louis Farrakhan, head of the militant Nation of Islam, held even before September the 11th, should resist assimilation by whites. 'We don't perceive ourselves as British Muslims', some claimed accordingly in the UK following the US attack on Afghanistan; 'we are Muslims who live in Britain.' It did not take long before a few ordinary Western-born and educated Muslims decided to be 'ruthless to the unbelievers', put on their deadly rucksacks and, though uncertain as to whether they should present themselves to Allah bearded or clean-shaved, turn into savage terrorists. Theirs must be now 'the dark-eyed houris, chaste as hidden pearls: a guerdom for their deeds'.

But by then the common identity and set of values, and together with it the political and moral centre, had been eroded in the name of multiculturalism. The notion of the whole was no longer there. The strings of Orpheus' lyre, stretched on the shell of a tortoise, have been taken apart, for each one of them can presumably produce the same divine music the lot of them did together.

Fragmentation has been heralded as the triumph of personal choice, the victory of the individual against the oppressive forces of the whole. But the liberation from the repressive restrictions of the past, the eternal, the universal and the essential, all of which, supplying the blueprint for our existence, shaped our minds and feelings, and determined our relationship with the world, has not led to the supreme affirmation of the individual. Nor has it freed man from discredited forms nor enabled him to chart a course in life as he thinks fit without guidance from any authority. To the dismay of its architects, the disillusioned *soixante-huitards*, freedom from absolute truths has, instead, delivered the individual into the arms of bankers and traders, and into those of his or her own self-obsession, the 'I', which, Johann Gottlieb Fichte, the German philosopher, maniacally asserted, is our only ultimate reality. Margaret Thatcher's dictum 'there is no such thing as society' diagnosed, indeed, the modern age's sole point of reference. Scornfully, Vladimir Mayakovsky could have pronounced once again 'I feel my "I" is too small for me.'

Personal choice in matters ranging from what beer we drink to what moral commitments we make was made possible by the multinationals themselves, those whom, as Wordsworth might have said, 'fate beyond the promise of their birth had glorified'. They challenged profoundly concepts such as cultural identity or tradition, whose place, they decided, is in the museum of Freaks and Oddities. What matters is 'personal choice' on which they bank in order to promote and sell what a local, and rather restrictive, political, religious or cultural practice would not have allowed them to. People, for them, are not divided along national, racial, ethnic, gender, sexual or religious lines, all remnants of a prejudiced past. What matters is only 'wealth creation', which, in turn, demands freedom for everyone to buy the multinationals' services and products, unhindered by considerations outside the flow of money.

Women, homosexuals and ethnic groups, Islamic or otherwise, all having considerable purchasing power, are, therefore, all valued customers, members of the world family, united in the consumption of beer, hamburgers, genetically modified food or cyber-porn. The latter, developing fast to the dismay of conservatism, which cannot accept the cultural product of its own free market revolution, has, of course, nothing to do with freedom of expression and everything with profits. Yet, pornography breaks at once both one more taboo and the control the State has over the life of the individual. Ironically, though the struggle to break through many barriers of repression has been led by the Left, it was the free market, instead, which managed to bring about, and in almost no time, more radical changes than the

Left could ever dream of except that we have all ended as nothing but postmodernism's unaccountable casualties of our unrealities and victims of the free market's onslaught of choice.

Unwilling to cross the boundaries of the self and the fixation on the drama of individual existence, the Ego, the 'seed of the apocalypse' according to Tao Te Ching, is not merely the bearer of nihilism, but of annihilation. While overwhelmed by his own insignificance and at the same time full of self-importance, man becomes, indeed, the primal force of self-destruction, the instigator of his own extirpation. Self-absorption, malignant and vicious, is the scarf of Isadora Duncan, the American pioneer of modern dance, around the neck of the new minorities which have emerged in disorderly queues of one. It is theta for thanatos in whose realm, postmodernism asserts, we have already entered. Man, a social, historical or linguistic artifact, without any essential qualities, is, it informs us, already 'dead'.

Thankfully, if we are lucky, in his graveyard we may pick a young widow – 'men', James Joyce said, 'like that. Love among the tombstones'. But rather unfortunately, we tend to be, as postmodernism reassures us, dead ourselves, dead as Queen Anne, indistinguishable from the furrows of erosion, forms dissolving into formlessness illuminated by fluorescent perfumes we wear to be noticed.

Freedom from absolute truths needs a context, moral and ethical, in order to give meaning to, and enhance, the life of the individual. But this is what the free market cannot provide. Yet a rudderless, mean world with no ideals worth living for, let alone dying for, a secular society without the ethical foundations which it ought to and should provide, and individuals who are expected to have faith in nothing, is a world that contains in itself the seeds of its destruction. Revitalised religious and political fundamentalism, exempt from intellectual influences, are intent on proving the point. The re-appearance of religion as a force determined to give people something to believe in, and this in a way that looks likely to redefine the political and social struggles as religious battles, is the inevitable result.

But nothing seems to bother us. Nothing can disturb our ataraxia that a 1989 Chateau Kirwan would not be able to settle. Engaged in an inner search for the aftershave that is really 'me', the Millennial Generation, successor of Generation X, is, like God, ultimately unconcerned. Looking 'for the face I had before the world was made', may well be, not just another form of, but the ultimate, illusion.

One day we may well find it, but this, sometimes, when spirits are low, does not look likely to happen before the fish on the fishmonger's stall smiles to the customer.

6. The Word 'Mother' Remains

As all members of an indescribable majority in search of an identity lost in time know, words are there only to disguise man's thoughts. This is the case now as much as it has been in the past, the time when, as George Burns, one of the USA's greatest comedians, tells us, sex was dirty and the air clean. Our communication with the world has, indeed, never intended to give the real picture, but only the one which is expected to produce the desired effects. Men, Darius, the Persian king, said a long time ago, lie when they intend to profit, and tell the truth for the same reason.

If one is to look the word in the eye, the inevitable conclusion is that words, used, misused and abused, can neither be trusted nor relied upon. 'Double-yoked with meaning and meaning's rebuttal', to quote Philip Larkin, they repress as much as, Foucault and Derrida or the linguist Emile Benvetiste held, they conceal. Telling the difference between real and unreal, essence and looks, true and false is, thus, as difficult as deciding on the merits of Damien Hirst's art. The postmodernist claim of their indistinguishability cannot, therefore, be easily opposed. The provenance of truth is unfathomable, abstruse, impenetrable, and words, particularly in days of absent certainties, do not help to clarify matters. Indeed, communication is there, just like history, only to distort rather than interpret our realities.

This being the case, manipulation and reformulation of reality, its creative reinterpretation and misrepresentation, is its denial in favour of an image that can neither be sustained nor relied upon. The world out there becomes an illusion, a fantasy which turns into the deceptive intermediary of our connection with reality, if not into the reality itself. Gone is the very ordinary reality as it is verified by the senses, too. Reality, the New Age claims, probably under the influence of too much meditation, has nothing objective about it, for the only reality is the reality we create and experience. In this reality, home-made and full of absent conflict, experiences, if they feel real and meaningful regardless of whether they can stand up to any rational analysis, are real and true.

Having no independent standing, the world outside the self does not even exist. Scepticism can, indeed, question anything, from the external world and human experiences to scientific inquiry and ethical considerations. Taken to its logical conclusion, it can almost convincingly make the case that the world, supplied with a geological record and memories of the past, was created only yesterday.

As Ferdinand de Saussure, the Swiss linguist, explained, meaning is lost because the 'signifier', the word, stands for the 'signified', the meaning or concept of the word, but it is not identical to it. The interiority of a mental image, its presence, cannot be united with the exteriority of the word, the representation of the image. The presence, indeed, is represented rather than presented, and representation can end up misrepresenting the represented. Words, in this sense, like everything else through which we present ourselves and make our statement to the world, everything that conveys meaning, messages and differences, have no meaning. Even if they had originally been filled with a meaning, they pass their 'best before' date as soon as their marriage to reality is consummated. They become the carriers of vaporous intentions.

Signifiers, Jacques Derrida held, have neither an essential connection to, nor can they reach, the signified. Words, cloaked by cultural codes, submerged in cultural assumptions and manipulated by interests, cannot provide the proof of a final meaning. They 'stand for' what they signify, but rather than the mirror image of the signified, they are the image of what we choose to see in it, or of what, Michel Foucault said, we are forced to see by the all-pervasive impersonal social controls. Thus perceived reality, internalised, creates its own reality just as it did for that Greek drinking party, whose bewildered guests, imagining they were at sea, threw the furniture of the house out of the windows to prevent their boat from capsizing. Just as the creation of language creates the self that creates language, reality is, thus, denied in favour of the language we use to interpret it and, in doing so, manipulates and reformulates reality itself.

The postmodernist thesis as expanded by Foucault, Derrida, Rorty, Lacan or Baudrillard and earlier by Barthes, abolished, thus, completely the distinction between essence and appearance, real and artificial, true and false. The Aristotelian view of 'all that is', the centrality of substance, the thingness of the thing has been violently dismissed. Wittgenstein's 'natural or ordinary certainty', this undisputed territory, which, as he said, enables us to go on believing that hell is not 'normal', and that the normal will someday return, is abandoned. Reality and man, products of words which, impregnated with ideological presuppositions render them meaningless, are obliterated from existence. 'We milk the cow of the world', the poet says, 'and as we do, we whisper in her ear, "you are not true".'

Reality, Baudrillard argued, has been replaced by a 'hyperreality' into which our social totality has sunk. It is nothing less than a mediated experience, which, effacing the difference between the real and the imaginary, no longer has any 'outside'. Even the self, the centred-ego, is illusory, Jacques Lacan, the French psychoanalyst and writer, has argued, for it, like all else, is the product of the new linguistic and communications reality, which, according to postmodernist thinkers, bears no relation to the system of simulation. The signifiers have no reference outside themselves; and meaning is endlessly deferred. Reality is just the image, true only to its own self. It may be Tuesday but as long as the mirror shows Sunday, it is Sunday.

In the vaporous, sexy world of their virtual reality, unable to lift the veil of image, individuals are no longer autonomous, self-conscious agents capable of determining their choices. Man, a 'construction' of forces beyond the self, caught in the spider's web of his culture, 'decentred', unable to actualise his nature, reconnect with his original purpose and determine himself, is no longer. He is, postmodernism claims, a pathetic, 'ironic' spectator of the system that denies him. The self, Jacques Derrida held, evaporates, disappears like smoke dissipating in the sky or, according to Foucault, 'like a face drawn in sand at the edge of the sea'. In this situation, Baudrillard gloomily pronounced, we are no longer permitted to isolate 'human nature as a fundamental variable' – we are, perhaps, as influential as the giant rats of Sumatra.

The liberation of the individual from intolerable universalisms has presumably not delivered the personal autonomy, the individuality it has promised. The weather reformers have not managed to produce a new, original winter. Interestingly, however, the 'death of man' is not the end of everything, for the subtitle to its announcement reassuringly reads: 'Business as usual'. Apparently, the situation is hopeless, but not so bad.

The uncertainty generated envelops the whole of our existence, for problems can be raised, as Murray Bookchin, the American intellectual eco-warrior, said, even by a moral axiom like 'thou shalt love thy neighbour as thyself.' One can in this sense legitimately ask what do you really mean by 'love', 'neighbour' or 'thyself'. In times that, for better or worse, no-one wants more common sense, Jacques Derrida can ask – as he did – what is the meaning of 'what': what happens to the hole after you eat the bagel, what happens to pure thought after the last man has emptied his veins of all blood? President Clinton, likewise, testifying to Kenneth Starr, asserted that 'it all depends on what the meaning of "is" is'. Texts, the reader-response theory asserts, have no meaning in themselves. Meaning is a mental construct concocted by the reader.

Concepts are often linguistically impenetrable. Samuel Beckett, the Irish-born playwright and novelist, striving to find fitting words to say what he wanted, ended up seeking fitting words 'so that the thing I am trying in vain to say may be tried in vain to be said'. Language, grossly abused to hide the will to power, often fails to create the meaning it purports, or it is expected to. In the marketing of ideas, it can also easily turn reality upside down. The killing of civilians in war is, in this sense, nothing to lose any sleep about – it is just 'collateral damage'. Slaughtering of the opposition is 'degrading the enemy'; and assassination of civilians by air-launched missiles just 'targeted killings'.

But this is not the failure of language. The causes of its distortion, the parasitic growth of a speech-oriented language, is the malformation of the human character. It is humans who are the transgressors. 'Lord', pleads George Seferis, the poet who ended his long diplomatic career in 1962 as Greece's ambassador to the UK, 'help us to keep in mind the causes of this slaughter: greed, dishonesty, selfishness, the desiccation of love ... bad habits, fraud and deceit, or even the selfish urge to reap reward from the blood of others.' Words like duty, honour, rectitude, sacrifice, virtue, solidarity, nobility or reverence, though humiliated and cursing – cursing, as Dante might say, 'God, their own parents, the human race, the time, the place, the seed of their beginning, and their day of birth' – still have a history, meaning and feelings. Though they often fall into disuse like maiden names, they still have a destination which gives, as poet Pablo Neruda put it, 'glass-quality to glass, blood to blood, and life to life itself'.

Hiding behind beef-witted words to deny reality altogether is not philosophical wisdom but hypocrisy. 'Words', Yannis Ritsos emphasised while trying to resist the erosion of a traditional world, 'fade with the years'; yet, 'the word mother remains.' Such words are 'outlets for a meeting, often postponed; but they are real when they insist upon the meeting'. The same goes for words such as love, friendship or integrity. They are what they mean to be rather than their prostituted version, the things themselves rather than their descriptors.

Likewise, situations answering to the name of global warming, homelessness and destitution, repression, loneliness, discrimination, racism, crime, unemployment, environmental degradation, foreign occupation or nuclear weapons are our reality, obscene, unspeakable and unthinkable. The barefoot citizens of Manshiyet Nasr, in Egypt, who jump over pools of raw sewage, sort through piles of rubbish in the company of cats, dogs and flies, buy shampoo in sachets and cigarettes singly rather than in packets and have nothing to hope for, certainly think so even if postmodernist thinkers may not. So will we when the unprincipled pursuit of profit, the religion of our time, may force us one day to produce what was previously abundant and free – oxygen for the atmosphere, water for the rivers and cold for the poles.

None of this is either an abstraction in the consciousness of the individual or a truth to be rejected because there are no universal truths. This sense of reality, as Horkheimer, Marcuse, Adorno, the Frankfurt School theorists, or John Kenneth Galbraith, the Canadian-born economist, insisted, cannot be presumed lost.

Our era cannot, however, accept such outrageous truths, the kind of truths which are certain to 'endure for centuries after my death, as (they) had endured for centuries before my birth'. Just as Emperor Amurath the Great, in the story of Evelyn Waugh, hanged the culprits and together with them two or three witnesses, we kill philosophical mythology and its eternal truths, and together with them their very real consequences which are being subjectivised.

This duplicity is hardly likely to win an Oscar in honesty. It is also unlikely to help the underprivileged, for since reality does not exist, nothing can change. What does not exist cannot change; and the corpse, as the Peruvian poet César Vallejo would have said, can go on dying.

Cynicism, now a family disease, tells us that nothing is good in itself, nothing is worth believing in as nothing is worth striving for. It follows that the only decent thing people can do under such circumstances is watch, be uninvolved, resign. The invitation to silence, the virtue of the dead, is made in the name of dignity and self-respect. But what they both conceal is a self-interest travelling incognito, the self-interest that underpins the contemporary solemn commitment to apathy and paves the way to resignation with all the excuses sophistication can buy. Disengaged, impotent, and hopeful that an invisible hand will avert the final catastrophe just before the end of time, or at least before the news of its impending arrival reaches the stock exchange, we can, thus, focus unerringly on our era's essential stylistic requirements, the outward form of a whim unfastened from the mind. Alternatively, we are free to articulate our discontent with acts of vandalism or terrorist attacks.

But cynicism is not a virtue. It is the squeal of impotence in sub-zero temperatures, the philosophy of spectators reflecting the grey void in the contemporary man's rectangular soul. The honest admission of Derrida, the coryphaeus of the postmodernist chorus, that he is not inspired by a concern that could 'by right be called ethical, moral, responsible etc' is, therefore, not all that impressive. He knew, he said, that his admission would give ammunition to his opponents. But he preferred that 'to the constitution of a consensual euphoria or, worse, a community of complacent deconstructionists, reassured and reconciled with the world in ethical certainty, good conscience, satisfaction of service rendered, and the consciousness of duty accomplished.' His tribute to honesty looks like a tribute to the dead of the two World Wars.

Reality may have disappeared from a world that feeds on illusions, the ideology of our time to which our inner selves relate. So may have whatever reflects the emotional and spiritual dimension of the human experience. No kindness, compassion or love for anything can fit in a reality for which nothing is real – love, incidentally, Iris Murdoch said, is 'the extremely difficult realisation that something other than oneself is real'.

Postmodernism in its French, dandified form, has highlighted the absurdities of modernism and raised some very important issues regarding reality, objectivity and truth which cannot be dismissed. But the price paid for these changes is a general disorientation. Its philosophy is the philosophy of resignation, apathy, disengagement, cynicism and fragmentation, and its critique of Reason, a snobbish display of intellect without virtue, has failed completely and utterly to challenge even the most repulsive practices of the modernism it criticises. Another absolute truth like those it decries, its thesis has not de-ideologised the contemporary world. It is itself an ideology, which demonstrates its falsehood just as Epimenides, the Cretan, did when he asserted all Cretans are liars.

As the cultural force that, as Terry Eagleton, the British academic, observed, sanctimoniously confirms and legitimates the status quo, postmodernism is for many the face of neo-conservatism, 'clever', as George Orwell would probably be happy to say once again, 'and yet inherently despicable'. Its frivolous and politically irresponsible attack on the rationalist and humanist ideals of the Enlightenment, Jürgen Habermas had said earlier, recalls the dark moments of counter-Enlightenment thought in Germany and more recent sinister intellectual and political currents. Its philosophy, Murray Bookchin pointed out, is bordering on outright nihilism and antihumanism leading to 'an appalling regression of rationality into intuitionism, of naturalism into supernaturalism, of realism into mysticism, of humanism into parochialism, and of social theory into psychology'. The Yellow Age may have come into consciousness with its own anti-ideological ideology, inviting us to accept the market-friendly and value-free one-dimensional definition of our existence.

But inevitably, postmodernism's scepticism, relativism, cynicism, irony, its dismissal of all truths, and, of course, its 'intellectualism', are also a thorn in the side of a conservatism craving a return to the standards which have done nothing but oppressed, controlled and dominated all those different from 'us'. Hence novelist Tom Wolfe, among others, denounced it as a 'neo-Marxist' philosophy, a 'Rococo Marxism, elegant as a Fragonard and sly as a Watteau'.

It looks, however, as if all this is history as postmodernism, unable to withstand the pressures of the new millennium, is fading into the background. The generation of the disillusioned that emerged in the post-1968 era and shaped its thinking has switched, as Umberto Eco, the Italian author of *The Name of the Rose*, acidly remarked, from Red Label to twelve-year-old Ballantine and then to single malt. The former '60s disillusioned radicals are yesterday's world. At any rate, the nature of life has made its claims on them. The death of Jean Baudrillard (2007), the last of its most brilliant exponents, after that of Jacques Derrida (2004), Jean-François Lyotard (1998), Gilles Deleuze (1995) and Michel Foucault (1984) marks, perhaps, our entering into a new philosophical era, the nature of which remains to be defined. Modernism has become modern once again but postmodernism will, perhaps, stay with us for a very long time, albeit not as the voice of a disillusioned generation. It will be there, instead, as the voice of the individual who cares about nothing but himself.

On the other hand, disillusioned for too long, we may just be ready to regain our illusions. Reality may have 'virtually disappeared' so that even our real names are probably not our real names. But whatever is out there will certainly need its redefinition by our time which, one can hope, will not be done by the religious fanatics on everybody's behalf.

Though not a book, life is still full of strange tales – strange, poet Jean Follain would say, 'in its curves and its volumes, its colours and adornments and shadows'.

7. A Knickers' Morality

The era which demanded purity of the soul as the prerequisite for experiencing the delights of eternal life, the time the soul looked contemptuously upon the body and the body's denial was enforced upon the individual has, of course, gone. Time, as Cervantes put it, is 'the devourer and consumer of all things'. Following the latest mental demolition of more sexual taboos, a process that started roughly at the same time professional footballers stopped using public transport for the Saturday match, outwardly the picture changed dramatically even further. 'No more shameless beds', in Kavafis' verse. 'No derisive shame for the form of his enjoyment'. The change, which horrified the conservatives, was a further step away from the hypocritical and repressive pre-permissive times, and another step, psychoanalyst Wilhelm Reich would have happily said, towards humankind's social and political liberation.

But the legacy of the previous era, despite the neuroses, the phobias, the guilt and the obsessions, the distortion and the falsification of human nature it causes, still lingers on. Centuries after the nuns used to wear shirts in the privacy of their baths to hide their bodies from God, the body, an intriguing mystery, still external to us, outside of ourselves as Sartre said, remains the unmasterable otherness. 'I was more familiar with Africa than my own body', Joe Orton, the English dramatist who was murdered in 1967, eutrapically confessed. More seriously, a young writer such as Sophie Hannah lamented only too recently 'the indignity of having a body'. Sexuality is apparently a matter of the mind.

This is the case though capitalism, aiming at the improvement of sales, rates and profits, has turned sex into a resource for consumption, a means to an end. Content with the illusory sexual gratification provided through images, we watch, read and fantasise about it, titillated rather than appreciative, aroused rather than satisfied, alienated rather than engaged. Commercialised and vulgarised, sexuality remains, as a result, once again largely a matter of the mind.

The old Christian morality, of which we are still prisoners, will not let sex move from the mind, where it dwells, to the body, where it belongs. Such a thing would be immoral. Morality, associated with sex, is, thus, still perceived in terms of what individuals do in their private life, the privacy of their bedrooms. Caught sauntering outside the existing framework of proper personal behaviour, they are pilloried by the tabloids, these self-appointed guardians of our morals. If above board in this respect, they are, of course, as white as a codfish's belly and as pure as the shepherds of Drury Lane when Drury Lane was still a meadow. The rules of the system are not all that many. They need, however, to be observed if the system's skill in putting its moral deficit to its best advantage is not to be tested. On this rests the maintenance of its moral authority, the preservation of the credibility of the reassurances conveyed by its vacant smiles, the concealment of its 'wide-branched indifference'. 'Honest' women, though very expensive, need to look honest. Hence the disavowal of the 'better element' when it blatantly disregards the club's rules.

Caught in the arms of this morality, president Bill Clinton felt obliged to repent, almost in tears, before American religious leaders because, as he said, he had 'sinned'. His 'sin' was an 'inappropriate' relation, not the bombing at the very same time of the 'chemical weapons' factory in Sudan which was not a chemical weapons factory, and the killing of a large number of innocent people for whom nobody in the West was able to spare a tear. Although a crime, partly responsible, as educator and linguist Noam Chomsky suggested, for the attack of September the 11th, neither the US president nor any moral crusader ever considered it a morally 'inappropriate' act, much less a sin. Power politics plainly has nothing to do with morality. The latter, John Calvin, the French Protestant theologian and reformer, held, is honoured as long as unlibidinous sex is restrained within the bounds of marriage and churchgoing is enforced on Sundays. Women, obviously, are not allowed to go to the office without knickers.

Good Christians, those who would not do anything decent unless their meanness is out of focus, can bomb, burn, destroy, rob, humiliate, exploit their fellow human beings, despoil the Earth, and commit the gravest acts of injustice as long as they appear to behave themselves sexually. For the Church, even political rebellion against the established order was not as bad as the free expression of a person's sexuality. But society is unwilling to oblige and meet Christian expectations on issues such as premarital sex, contraception, teenage pregnancies, masturbation, abortion, divorce, homosexuality, pornography or nudism.

In the whirlwinds of a moral panic, accentuated by things such as the disclosure of Janet Jackson's tit on television, a new breed of Christians, thus, felt forced to launch their counterattack. 'Moral politics', committed to the 'purely moral' as Nicole Kidman is to fame, was born. According to its personal moral hygiene, it is not the way a person behaves towards his fellow human beings that is important but the way he steers his sexuality, controls it, indeed, suppresses it in order to join President George W. Bush's 'elite moral community'. 'I have carefully avoided inviting any beautiful, attractive, farouche young women', the American playwright and poet Louis Simpson noted entertainingly, as if he were interested in Bush's project; 'but the Vicar of Dunstable is coming ... and the Calvinist Spiritual Chorus Society.'

Virtue in this respect is the moral strength to resist the desires of the flesh. 'The body belongs to Christ', I read in an Evangelist website, virtuous as cold oatmeal; sex is an 'addiction'; Christians have to remain 'sexually pure'. As an official of the Festival of Light clarified for our benefit some time ago, the body is a mere nothing in relation to pure spirit. 'If God had intended us to prance about in the nude', he thundered, 'we should all have been born naked.' Such purity is, presumably, what makes the moralists' inner selves, who for a long time have not felt so well, feel a little bit better. It also helps to make carpet bombing, relished against those who threaten 'human rights and cosmopolitan values', appear to be as morally objectionable as a storm.

Betraying our sexuality is presumably God's will. Paul articulated the point when, in his letters to the Corinthians, he warned them: 'Don't be fooled; neither fornicators and idolaters, nor adulterers, self-abusers and homosexuals...shall inherit the Kingdom of God.' As forcefully, Peter, with the look of sexual deprivation all over him, commanded the faithful: 'Abstain from the lusts of the flesh which are at war with the soul.' Ever since, the repression of sexuality by the sexecutioners has been the flag of the religious counter-revolution, the yardstick of the new, deformed morality, which even the Soviets, too eager to protect the innocence of their eyes, were quick to emulate. Grotesque though it is, this kind of morality in rather fearful forms was adopted by the new guardians of the truth, those who, pursuing a 'new spiritual awakening', turned sexuality, the symbolic embodiment of all earthy pleasures, into the enemy to be crushed as commanded by the inerrant and infallible Bible, the keystone to their truth.

The queue was joined by the Islamic fundamentalists. Recalling the ethos of a long passed barbaric era, they attacked consumer hedonism and modernist decadence, the Godless, materialistic and soulless western society. Right and wrong is for them as clear and unambigious as right and left. Needless to say, the focus of their attack is the public worship of female flesh, 'shamelessness and fornification', 'the overload of information', as Shaykh Riyad Nadwi, director of the Oxford Cross Cultural Research Institute, said, 'men receive from, for instance, protruding cleavages and legs clad in these silk stockings dangling from beneath short skirts.' A woman, presumably, has to cover herself from head to toe just to hide her awra, i.e., the part of her body that arouses sexual desires in men. Women, Allah's Messenger clarified for our benefit, advance and retire 'in the shape of a devil'. Hence 'anything that is deemed to stir the passions or that may lead towards temptation and thus the sin of adultery' is forbidden. This includes even 'lustful gazes from either male or female towards each other'.

With virginity being the highest asset a woman could possess, there is no crime as despicable as a woman's losing it before marriage. Controlling the innate, natural and instinctive sexual desires and their joy is the ultimate objective of Islam's moral police. When married, people can, of course, enjoy sex, but this only means, as Imam Ghazali, the greatest of all Islamic scholars, explained, that a woman should keep herself clean at all times so that the man can enjoy her at will. A woman is, for the Islamic moralists, nothing but an instrument for providing carnal pleasure to man. The Islamic moral law, likewise, condemns masturbation as an 'abominable and wicked act', oral sex as 'a disgusting western practice', and so on. The Islamic moral code, the Sha'ria, includes instructions uttered by God Himself regarding other vital matters such as circumcision, shaving the pubic region, clipping the nails, bathing after sexual intercourse or cutting the moustaches short. Allah has certainly an eye for detail.

Embracing a form of faith-cum militancy, the Islamic legions have thus taken the front line in the battle for the reinstatement of moral virtues, those which the open expression of our sexuality has driven to the margin, and the defence of their faith. In doing so, they are obliged, as the Moroccan-Dutchman who murdered film-maker Theo van Gogh said in his trial, to 'cut off the heads of all those who insult Allah and his Prophet'. They were obviously as obliged to riot across Europe when cartoons of the prophet appeared in a newspaper.

I cannot help comparing here this kind of approach to that of the Greeks who, even in their Christian days, would yield neither to God nor to the world. 'You know, if you weren't the Holy Virgin', Kazantzakis tells us the aggravated Cretan shepherd shouts at the First Lady just to give her a taste of his feelings, 'I'd teach you a lesson with the handle of this pitchfork here.' He did not do so, for the man was, of course, full of reverence for her. Evidently less respectful, the late Barba Costantis, my neighbour in Atsitsa, on Skyros island, did not mince his words when his goats showed more independence than he would have liked them to. He verbally abused the Virgin, whose fault all this naturally was, as if she were a whore who had cheated him to the bone.

Developments could have hardly taken a different turn after US president George W. Bush locked himself in what he described as a cosmic struggle between good and evil. Banalised and absolutised, the 'enemy', president Bush's 'evil', became then the enemy of our 'civilised values'; and the war against it turned out to be as noble as the war on illiteracy or drugs. Its moral purpose is, however, as vibrant as the pulse of Stonehenge's ruins, and its effectiveness as powerful as pills against earthquakes. But religion has, as a result, emerged as a new global force determined to take us back to the golden age of bubonic plagues and monks.

Sexual freedom discourages religiosity, for those who can achieve ekstasis in sex do not need the church. As Erich Fromm, the German-born Jewish-American psychoanalytic humanist, rather irreverently submitted, the sexual orgasm can produce a state similar to the one produced by trance. But equally true, the free expression of a person's sexuality does not affect morality any more than watches made to tell the time, the temperature and also the altitude in any part of the world; and morality has nothing to do with submission to the will of God. Yet the 'Wall of Virtue' erected by the 'gray-grown' Christian morality, which, as Emma Goldman, the American radical feminist, said in 1913, enslaves the spirit of man, is convenient: it leaves the field wide-open to the disciplined and unimpeded pursuit of self-interest.

Indeed, beyond the obvious and the trivial, the Judaeo-Christian religion is based on the advancement of the interests of the faithful and/or their God. What matters here is not actions but the declared intentions, the latter being viewed as the only foundation of virtue and the ultimate moral evaluation of any action. Moral is not what is good in itself or what is judged as good by some objective standards of goodness, but what is good and right for 'us', a means, in other words, to the attainment of 'our' ends. Obscene and vicious practices look, as a result, as if they are determined by a moral imperative, the absolute and incontestable word of God as given to us by his appointed representatives, the authority of the untouchable. Men may slay, ravish, and destroy for His glory, but the motive condones, even consecrates the act. God himself gave the lead in this respect.

He 'struck down every first-born in Egypt, from the first-born of Pharaoh on his throne to the first-born of the captive in the dungeon, and the first-born of cattle' so that 'there was not a house in Egypt without its dead'; or He killed forty-two children just because they made fun of Elisha, the prophet. When He did not want to bother about such trivial things, He asked others, instead, to exterminate His and their enemies, which, following their God's will, they did: 'they utterly destroyed all that was in (Jericho), both man and woman, young and old, and ox and sheep, and ass, with the edge of the sword.' This savagery has nothing immoral about it. The place of love, which is supposed to be the foundation of Biblical ethics, is taken by religious intolerance, hatred and viciousness. 'I, the Lord your God, am a jealous God', He tells the faithful in the Old Testament. 'I punish the children of those who hate me for the sins of their fathers to the third and fourth generations.' Dropping 'sinners' from helicopters would, indeed, have been a more compassionate and merciful act. What follows is cruelty, deceit and murder on a massive scale in the interests of the Lord and his supporters.

Even Christ, the man who represented the human, civilised face of the Jewish religion, though he preached love for one's enemies, did not mince his words on other occasions: 'I haven't come', he said according to Matthew, 'to bring peace to the earth. I've come with a knife. I've come to set a man against his father, a daughter against her mother, a daughter-in-law against her mother-in-law, and a man's enemies will be under the same roof. Whoever loves his father or mother more than he loves me is not worthy of me.' That was, of course, the case until Christianity won its battle against its enemies.

Nonetheless, the pursuit of self-interest had not for a long time needed God's presence in secret meetings, divine strategic plans or a command structure headed by Him. The process had largely kept theology out of politics. Humans could do well after all without God's help as the Holocaust and Hiroshima can testify. But the emergence of the populist and vulgar religious and political Right in the last quarter of the twentieth century changed it all. 'History', as Russian novelist Boris Pasternak noticed, 'moves as invisibly in its incessant transformations as the forest in the spring.'

What seems to have changed it all is apparently God's change of heart. Having concluded that being concerned only about knickers in this world and business administration in the hereafter gives no real job satisfaction, or, alternatively, that Satan had, in His absence, taken too many liberties, God decided He had to step in to the affairs of His creation in person. One would have thought that the poor, oppressed and disadvantaged would have instantly called a press conference to announce the good news. Instead, it was born-again Christian George W. Bush who stepped in and reportedly said: 'God told me to strike at al-Qaeda and I struck them, and then he instructed me to strike at Saddam, which I did.' Satan had been dealt a blow as confirmed by Lt General William Boykin, Bush's deputy undersecretary for defence in charge of pursuing Osama bin Laden. The 'war on terror', he said before he was forced to eat his words, was a battle with Satan splendidly won by the American troops.

Christian fundamentalism has challenged postmodernist values and called for a return to the defining Bible-based principles of religion whose absolute authority and literal truth are wholly and unconditionally endorsed. It has not, however, challenged either the individualism on which postmodernism thrives or the self-interest which it serves. The greed of the fat cats or the drive towards the domination of the world by the US is thus carried out with the blessing of Jesus Christ, our personal Lord and Saviour. 'God is on our side.' 'Our side' is the American evangelical Christians, about a third of all Americans, split between Pentecostals, traditional Methodists, Baptists, Presbyterians, Anabaptists, Lutheran confessionalists and many others whose creeds are incomprehensible both to Europeans and also to Americans living in large urban centres.

Most of them are ultraconservative, anti-democratic, anti-humanist, anti-foreign, anti-abortion, anti-women, anti-labour, anti-welfare, anti-tax and pro-death penalty. And they all love freedom – the freedom to possess and use firearms, to force the world to remove all obstacles to their trade or to send their troops wherever 'evil' threatens American interests. In a survey carried out in the spring of 2004, 71 per cent of the evangelists polled said they would vote for reborn Christian George W. Bush. Voting against George Bush, Republican Congressman Tom Cole of Oklahoma told supporters, would be a vote for Osama bin Laden.

At once provincial and messianic, the Christian fundamentalists under the guidance of its chaplain-in-chief George W. Bush, the president whom Michael Moore renamed Jesus W. Christ, have, accordingly, split the universe between 'good' and 'bad', 'right' and 'wrong', the realm of God and the realm of Satan – one hankers for the time president Bush was guarding Texas against the Vietcong. The Gospel of the new, McDonaldised religion offers no other alternatives. It is either black or white. Their eschatological expectation is of an apocalyptic end amid a cosmic disaster that will turn water to blood until Jesus Christ makes a second coming, as a warrior this time, to overthrow the anti-Christ, whose forces assemble in the Middle East. The cosmic battle between the two is bound to end, of course, as in Hollywood films, with the victory of Christ and the setting up of the kingdom of God. Incidentally, St John's Book of Revelation on which they base their prediction describes the anti-Christ as the political ruler of the whole Earth, whose unified social, economic and religious system dominates the world. This is hardly the description of Osama bin Laden.

It follows that opposition to the US president, either domestic or international, cannot but be opposition to the will of God, a rejection of 'freedom, the Almighty's gift to every man and woman in the world', as president George W. Bush explained for our benefit. Incidentally, as Pennsylvania University professor Jonathan Steinberg noticed, the word 'freedom' does not figure in the Judaeo-Christian God's vocabulary. 'We are hated', General Boykin said, 'because we are a nation of believers ... a Christian nation.' The main feature of this 'Christian nation' is, however, greed, presented in the mega-churches as a Christian virtue – the evangelists' 'prosperity preaching' which tells the faithful that 'God wants us all to be super-rich right now'. Ann Coulter, the political commentator Al Franken called 'the reigning diva of the hysterical right' or 'the hysterical diva of the reigning right', took this call to new heights. She wrote: 'God says, "the Earth is Yours. Take it. Rape it. It's yours".' In the same vein, a Californian bumper sticker, popular just before the Iraq war, instructed president Bush to 'kick their Ass: steal their Gas.' The popular German actor and playwright Xaver Kroetzz might be forgiven if he were to reiterate his 'thank God I am not American.'

Under such circumstances, nothing 'our side' does can ever be morally wrong. Prewar sanctions against Iraq, according to UNICEF, led before the war to the death of more than 500,000 children under the age of five. Yet US Secretary of State Madeleine Albright did not see anything morally reprehensible about such a policy, which the UN's Humanitarian coordinator Denis Halliday, said, 'satisfies the definition of genocide'. 'The price', Albright replied when asked, 'is worth it.' Ariel Sharon, the Israeli prime minister, aided the massacre of 2,750 civilians in Sabra and Shatila, sent his tanks to ruin Jenin, and kept grabbing Palestinian land. Again, the indiscriminate slaughter of noncombatants or his supporters' banditry had nothing to do with morality – it is just necessary action in the interests of civilised values, albeit emancipated from every value.

'Actions', as George Orwell wrote in The Survival of the Adversary Culture, 'are held good or bad, not on their own merits but according to who does them, and there is almost no kind of outrage – torture, the use of hostages, forced labour, mass deportations, imprisonment without trial, forgery, assassinations, the bombing of civilians – which does not change its moral colour when it is committed by "our" side.' Take a different view and you have to explain why water is wet.

The story was not any different in Abu Ghraib and Guantánamo Bay or earlier, in Vietnam, where American military forces carried out mass executions, bombed civilians, defoliated half the country, poisoned its inhabitants with nerve gas and Agent Orange, carried out rape and torture, burned villages, shot children, threw prisoners out of helicopters and cut off the ears of people both alive and dead, keeping them as mementos and trading them for cans of beer. Or when the Americans were happy to back up corrupt, murderous cliques: Samosa in Nicaragua, Papadopoulos in Greece, Pinochet in Chile, Savimbi in Angola, Ngo Dinh Diem in Vietnam or the Shah of Iran. Such an atrocious policy was not considered to be immoral because morality is preoccupied with the tightness of vaginal walls.

In this sense, there is nothing immoral, either, in deceiving and manipulating public opinion or lying to the country and to the world in the interests of power politics as long as you oppose gay marriages. The 'serious and current' threat posed by Iraq if I can mention again the unmentionable, this ludicrous story based on what Hans Blinx, the UN chief weapons inspector called 'fabricated' evidence, is only too familiar.

'Iraq', Tony Blair, the British prime minister also known as the 'armed priest', told the House of Commons before the war, 'has continued to produce chemical and biological agents, has military plans for the use of chemical and biological weapons, (and) command and control arrangements in place to use chemical and biological weapons.' The latter included '10,000 litres of anthrax; a far-reaching VX nerve agent programme; up to 6,500 chemical munitions; at least 80 tons of mustard gas, and possibly more than 10 times that amount; botulinum toxin and a host of other biological poisons; and an entire Scud missile programme. All this while Saddam 'had sought significant quantities of uranium from Africa' to proceed with his nuclear armaments, and also while there was good intelligence that he had 'trained al-Qaeda members in bomb-making and poisons and deadly gases.' On the strength of what was presented as good intelligence, Blair further informed the nation that Iraq's lethal weapons 'could be activated within 45 minutes.' Goebbels, who in 1939 told the world that Poland was about to attack Germany, would have been proud of him.

As a result, and as God, the maker and enforcer of a moral law tailored to suit 'our' interests, has decreed, hundreds of thousands of Iraqi soldiers and civilians were massacred by the rivers of Babylon, their country was devastated, millions turned into refugees, and the country's rich oilfields, the world's second largest oil reserves, were delivered to multinationals. But for the Knight of the Flaming Sword and all those unable to weep with their own eyes, such tragedies, rather than a moral outrage, are 'inevitable' acts performed in His name, even charitable acts.

The consequences of lies – 'lies to last you a lifetime' as Nazim Hikmet, the first and foremost modern Turkish poet would have said – that annihilate the moral instinct in the First World, and the 'collateral damage', measured in unaccountable deaths and devastation in lands where pain is habitually the host, are the acceptable cost of the fight against 'evil'. Just like scientific enquiry, which since Descartes has been separated from ethics, the morals of power, its ends and means, the death it spreads with its conquests have nothing to do with morality. Yet, only too eager to turn self-deception into his home, succumbing, as Aeschylus would say, to the 'smooth delusion's flattering smile', Tony Blair hailed the American 'values' as 'the universal values of the human spirit'. 'The purveyors of death', writer Daniela Dahn, co-founder of the East German Democratic Renewal opposition movement in 1989, exclaimed, 'have been allowed to portray themselves as champions of western values.'

Likewise, beyond the moral scrutiny of our culture, are the grossly unfair trading rules of the World Trade Organisation, labelled by a United Nations-appointed study group as a 'nightmare' for developing countries, the vast wealth and power amassed by the few, and the poverty and the parallel disempowerment of the many or the planet's botching up. 'Infectious greed', a term used by Alan Greenspan, former chairman of the US Federal Reserve, rather than a virus, is, instead, a virtue in a world in which the desire for enrichment defines the national psyche; and rather than being denounced, it is celebrated.

Indeed, the brave new Christian soldiers, addressing themselves in the UK to the new master race of bankers, lawyers and media types, the 'gin and Jags' Christians who are looking for God 'the cool way', would hardly be expected to do anything else. A system that, in its moral numbness, views the accumulation of wealth as an important measure of success does not leave much margin for different personal choices. Greed and voracity are presumably as good as the laws of pure symmetry.

In the same spirit, avaricious chief executives with photos of their wives on their desks and a condensed version of the ten commandments for quick reference, have diverted staggering wealth from shareholders to themselves by the acquisition of stocks without relation to performance, the subversion of accounting standards and audits, and a host of value-destroying takeovers. 'Bank robbers, ' Jeffrey Cramer, the assistant US attorney in Chicago, said at the opening of the trial of newspaper publisher Conrad Black and three associates from Hollinger International, 'are masked and they use guns. Burglars wear black clothing and use crowbars. These men are dressed in ties and wear suits.' It is the latter who are able to appropriate truly amazing amounts of money to support a lifestyle ordinary people cannot even imagine.

Travelling first class and, therefore, a quality above suspicion, and yet obscene, distorted, and inhuman, morality, as it is understood, is nothing more than the morality of vested interests supporting an unjust system which protects the powerful against the weak and the rich against the poor. Sexual repression, thriving on duty carefully circumscribed by the ideology of monogamic fidelity, Marcuse held, strips sexuality of its playfulness and spontaneity. At the same time, its false, hypocritical, values have justified everything, from colonialism and imperialism to wars, the exploitation of the poor, the ravaging of the earth's natural resources, the degradation of life. They have filled the air with the scent of stale cabbage. 'Civilised life', Kropotkin, the Russian anarchist, said, has become 'a huge lie'. We accustom ourselves and our children to the practice of a double-faced morality and we cheat ourselves with sophistry. 'Hypocrisy and sophistry', inevitable as singing is to opera, which, Claude Debussy, the French composer, complained, is always too much, 'become the second nature of civilised man.' Rachel, in a Virginia Woolf novel, reached the same conclusion – 'nobody ever said a thing they meant', she decided, 'or even talked of a feeling they felt.'

Hence Nietzsche's call to his fellow human beings to undermine morality by exposing its non-moral basis, and rationality by exposing its non-rational basis, or the absurdities of the Marquis de Sade, the French nobleman and writer who forced a Parisian prostitute to watch him masturbating over a crucifix.

Moist like grass left out on a rainy night, Melissanthi, the Greek existential poetess, more subtly pencilled: 'every time I sinned, it was as though a door had opened.'

8. Rich in Zeroes

The age of honest talk, brown bread and wholesome wine has sunk into oblivion. Though some old people, those who, as Scottish poet Douglas Dunn said, 'know no fashions, copy nothing but their minds' and 'long ago, gave up looking in mirrors', may still possess them, the old qualities are also gone. Nothing in them can excite modern curiosity.

Little in our age which, like some currencies, is rich in zeroes, can take us beyond the freedom to have needs, those hinged on lifestyles. It is these needs that take priority over life, determine our existence, fill the gap between the moment and eternity. To meet them, we spend our life doing what we really do not want to be doing to earn the money to buy what we do not really need. Our time, health and leisure, traditions, institutions and social formations, even our life stories, blood, smiles, kidneys or eggs and sperm are offered willingly in exchange for the appropriate remuneration which will give us access to all things money can buy. But in the process we are consumed at the expense of everything else that matters: our relations with the people we love, the connection with our inner self and our body, the bonds with our community, the links with our purpose, with all things, which as Kurt Vonnegut, the American novelist, said, 'make your soul grow'. What is left is 'fun', reality shows which the system happily provides in unlimited quantities.

In the eastern provinces of the twenty-first century, which though uninvited arrived punctually, our entire lifestyle is, indeed, in a state of crisis. In the effort to make it in the way the system demands, trapped in its web of subliminal influences and chained down by our expectations, we have stopped being masters of our own selves. The increasing alienation, first of all, from our instinctual desires and the loving part of ourselves, and then from the world, is the inevitable result. What follows is loneliness and slow death, the death of the spirit. 'Hands we have never touched', as Greek poet Themelis put it, 'die out of loneliness, and dreams we have never seen, from lack of light.'

Cut off from all that gives meaning to our lives, we have nothing to which we can relate apart from our own selves. We are not at ease with our neighbours or colleagues, but with the characters of The Simpsons and of Coronation Street. In the carbuncled cities, the cage of our reality, we do not even know who our next door neighbours are. We double-lock our front doors and avoid talking to strangers – 'don't smile', a friend walking with me in New York advised me, 'they'll arrest you.' People are, indeed, our strangers, who nevertheless share something fundamental with us: our loneliness, the desertification of our existence, the lack of meaningful connections and also sophisticated burglar alarms to protect the void against intruders.

The personal community people were born into has become almost extinct – we live, novelist Joseph Conrad said, as we dream – alone. Nobody would grace us even with his enmity – we do not seem to have enemies any longer. Our 'friends' are not those we know but the digital citizens of the cybernetic superreality – even adultery is becoming virtual, developing in cyberspace as we discovered when a man asked for a divorce giving as grounds for it his spouse's online affair with a paramour. Our associates are people about whom we know nothing, people who exist as bearers of professional and social roles rather than autonomous human beings and are valued for 'what' as opposed to 'who' they are. What used to be our community, whether this community is the family, the village, the clan or the nation, has been dissolved or rather replaced by Vodafone's 'largest mobile community' or MySpace, Rupert Murdoch's social-networking website. In it, the 'us' imperceptibly dissolves, it is no longer 'us', individuality is obliterated and identity confused. As conscious of our existence as a post office box is of itself, we end up alienated from all our subjective realities and disconnected from the meaning and purpose which bring communities together.

Alienation from our cities is not a brand new phenomenon. Its beginning goes back, perhaps, to that morning when Charles Baudelaire, the nineteenth century French poet, looked out upon the billboards of Paris, 'that vast cemetery that is called a great city', and felt an immense disgust. It is, however, growing as life becomes more depersonalised, discourteous, unpleasant, monotonous and lonely, and as death, Greek poet Costas Cariotakis said, has a new face, 'the filthy, commonplace streets with all their great, splendiferous names'. Alienated from the sources of social power, without any influence on our overall destiny, and poor in terms of relations and real communication, we also end up alienated from the world. Or, as contemporary Greek thinker Cornelius Castoriades put it, we end up belonging to it, not as adults, but infantiles who have replaced the private father with the social anonymous father, the market and its designer goods which enable us to forge an identity and let the world know 'I'm like that.'

The 'human moment', defined by a Harvard psychiatrist as 'an authentic psychological encounter that can happen only when two people share the same physical space', is disappearing from our lives. This is the case even when two people do share the same house. Television has ensured that we have moved from the solitude of the single to that of the married life, to what James Joyce called 'the silent marriage' in which the realm of inarticulate monosyllables passes as meaningful communication. 'We devised a signal for the hereafter, a whistle for each other', Eugenio Montale, the Italian poet, wrote with a rather morbid sense of humour. 'I'm trying it now, hoping we're already dead not knowing.' If Rubén Darío, the Nicaraguan poet, founder of Spanish modernism, was right when he said that there is 'no greater affliction than conscious life', this, of course, may well be a blessing.

Relations are no longer valued – few carry on playing happy families after dinner. 'Dedicated bachelorettes' and 'serious singletons', happy to prepare breakfast for themselves and the cat, do not even look forward to close personal relations. Such relations are associated with duties, and duties are disagreeable because they stand in the way of the love affair we have with ourselves. Though the trend might have been reversed recently, weddings have, as a result, halved, and divorces trebled. At the same time, the proportion of children born outside marriage quadrupled within the space of a generation: two fifths of them are born out of wedlock. Nearly a third of all households in the UK are people living alone – the size of the average household is now 2.4 down from 3.1 in the early sixties.

Parenthood, or even emotional commitments, are seen as a burden to be avoided. It seems that either we can no longer stand each other, or are so full with our 'I', and so enchanted by its looks, that we do not need anybody else close to us. The time when marriage was the job a woman was destined to have is over – marital ties look to many like a marital chain. Able to build a life detached from everything including our own selves, we end up as a seed, to quote novelist and poet D.M. Thomas, 'cast on stony ground'. Sure enough of our personal identity to order a cappuccino, we are, thus, like everyone else but even more so, masters of our fate.

Love does of course exist but in films and books. The reality is different. 'Next time we commit love', Canadian novelist Margaret Atwood recommends, 'we ought to choose in advance what to kill.' Yet the first casualty is often sexuality itself, for the suppression of instincts plus their simultaneous illusory satisfaction in the heat of the electric nights and the Net's minimal reality has transferred sexuality from the body to the brain. Sex, an issue never raised in front of 'your wife or your servants' as we were told in fiercely official tones not all that long ago, is still a matter of the mind.

The growing disharmony between parts of ourselves, the split, in particular, between mind and body, damages both as the body atrophies and the mind gets ill. Man is broken, as the nineteenth century English social critic John Ruskin said, into small fragments and crumbs of life. He is divided into mere segments of man, living only portions of his nature, in allotments of his culture. Considering the different roles we often assume in our compartmentalised life, we may not even be the same person on each occasion – there is a different face for each part of it. Hence the stress and our dependence on specialists increases; hence also the hours of work we need to do to earn the money to pay for their services.

The concept of man, 'an invention of recent date', seems bound, at least according to postmodernist theory, to disappear altogether, its face dissolving in the eidolon, the unsubstantial apparition.

The very notion of the individual chivalrous self, so central to the Enlightenment's philosophy of human rights, is, indeed, crumbling. Even civility is giving up the ghost, for life, having grown indefinitely vast, no longer has the interlinkage that holds it together. We eat like chickens, anywhere, on the tube, in the car or on the road, we copulate in public lavatories, we go to war in distant lands and bomb them from the safety of distance. Though invisible, and somehow unacknowledged, it is, however, the soul, 'travelling on the decks of decayed ships', that suffers most. In the spiritual emptiness of our day, it has become, as in George Seferis' poetry, 'the image of a form that the sentence to everlasting bitterness has turned to stone.'

Painfully aware of it, unfulfilled because 'my soul is dying', fed up with years of greed, and tired of even the megawealth which 'success' has produced, many, particularly senior executives, follow in the steps of Gauguin or Kandinsky, who abandoned their career as a stockbroker and lawyer respectively in order to paint. Stepping out of lucrative careers into the world of commerce, law and finance, they start a new and balanced life in low paid, but fulfilling, situations in which they are in charge of their own destiny and do something validated by society rather than the market. 'Downshifting' is becoming a sort of fashion, some say a social movement, in the new millennium – the numbers of those who joined the UK's 'quiet revolt against the culture of getting and spending' reached 2.6m in 2004 against 1.7m in 1997. Yet they are looked upon with utter disbelief by those who carry the free market's flag. 'How can our glorious King Mithridates', poet Kavafis asks in astonishment on their behalf, 'possibly occupy himself now with Greek poems? In the midst of war – just imagine, Greek poems.' In other times, less peculiar, these people would be called honest.

The time when we felt we had something in common with each other – common ethical, social, environmental, cultural or economic concerns, or common aims, hopes and fears – seems to be over for good. There are not even joint interests to defend. Few march for a safe, and even fewer for a better, world. British prime minister Blair and US president Bush have made sure that, no matter how numerous we may be, we can safely be ignored. Even the occasional interest in soft ecological issues is no longer there. Perhaps demanding more and more power for less and less has shown its limitations, as has the enthusiasm about low-flow faucets and high-mileage cars. Pessimism, Francis Fukuyama said just before the end of the century, has turned into something of a fashion.

In tune with it, the academia, absorbed by the academic commercial establishment and without the moral courage that earned Voltaire persecution, cudgelling and banishment, resigned itself to an ironical, unamiable emotional detachment from what is commonly perceived as life. The language of its members, anhydrous and tedious, cerebrally dull and barely comprehensible, seem to be in tune only with their ostentations. The pains and the pleasures of life, those experienced by simple folks, do not seem to touch them; the word 'soul', Paul Tillich, the German-born theologian and philosopher sadly reflected, is forbidden in their context. It has shut its door and answers no calls. As Jürgen Habermas pointed out, independent thinkers such as Marx, Kierkegaard and Nietzsche still play a larger part in the world of ideas than academic philosophers. So do people like Darwin and Freud.

The unserviceable dreams, those abstract notions of a humanity reconciled with its own self, undocumented as they are and without references, are not for us. They are for the useless, the poets, the romantics, the dimwits who light candles to the sun or the 'hysterical humanists', as Raymond Tallis, a neurologist, said. Dreamers, just like grammarians, another dwindling breed in these hard times of a monosyllabic intelligence, have become an endangered species.

The spirit that guides the flesh and upholds the values of humanity, the breathing of our hopes, our connection with virtue, the universe or the harmony of cosmos is no longer there. The smoke we see is not produced by a fire – it is only its simulation. With the attachment to the wonders and the nobility of life gone, man has ceased to be at one with the eternal rhythms, his sensitivity. Concepts such as self-consciousness and self-realisation are denied, and language is deprived of all meaning. In the field of life's grey anonymity, the 'place of disaffection', to use T.S. Eliot's description, at the mercy of our unbridled individualism, and yet free, free to dye our hair the colour of despondence or celebrate Christmas with a takeaway pizza, we can no longer connect with anything apart from our own needs. It follows that no person has any right to expect support from his fellows. It is the state and commercialised services that are expected to provide now what people used to give each other.

Civil society, defined as the web of social relations founded upon reciprocity and voluntarism that individuals establish among themselves within the context of groups or communities, has almost disappeared. To survive now we have to construct our own personal community in which the respect promised to us the moment we were born will not be denied. Should we fail to, we will have to talk to each other through our T-shirts, if, of course, we have something to say – 'the day', poet Anagnostakis prophesied, 'will come when we'll have nothing left to say.' Or, we will communicate with others through our personal affairs agents.

Montesquieu, the eighteenth century French political philosopher, made the point that one of the outstanding features of tyranny was the isolation of its subjects from each other through mutual fear and suspicion. Fear and suspicion, which only a generation ago we thought we had banned, is still around – fear of hooligans, burglars, rapists, murderers, terrorists; and so is suspicion – that of strangers, including our neighbours, men kind to our children or people of other races. The cities of lost content, in whose streets only the supermarkets' tills are alert, know no longer of the whole.

The situation is almost desperate not just in large cosmopolitan centres, but even in smaller places as well. A poll sampling thousands, conducted by the psychiatric clinic of the university of Athens, revealed that an amazing thirty-one per cent of the population is stressed, depressed and suffers from psychosomatic illnesses. Ten per cent of Athenians have at some point considered suicide. This is not the celestial city to which the free market economy, flying on the wings of science and technology, is supposed to have taken us. This is the negative of the dream, a frightening world. Our time has met its Cannae in the market's culture of disposable nappies, cars, husbands, children, feelings, conscience. The individual is left entirely on his or her own to cope with the social epidemic, ready even to blame his or her own self for failure to do so.

Yet, and though so perishingly close to the edge, we want more, more of the same, more uselessness and confusion, for, as it seems, we have not got enough. More of the same presumably represents quality, the quality which, measured by biomarkers, can be obtained at the nearest place: Prozac to enhance our mood if we are feeling down, Ecstasy to be happy and Viagra to uplift the spirit.

Modernism, in its madness, plain and blunt, bald as an egg, gives us something only to take it back with interest. We are on our own and in debt for it. Under pressure to prevail and succeed, shine and impress, acquire and prosper, conquer and master, fascinated by our own selves and divorced from our community, and also restrained, as Freud said, by the need to work to earn a living, by the imposition of a monogamous relationship, and by the established system of law and order, we remain exposed to the hissing winds of life. Resourceless and impotent, we watch the increasing isolation and evanescence of the individual and his or her disempowerment, the degradation of the environment or the destruction of cultural diversity, the concentration of power in fewer and fewer hands.

Confronted with such a dismal-looking picture, modernity's zero as a paradigm, the practical mind, tempered by mind-conditioners, has, thus, no alternative but to seek fulfilment elsewhere, in the satisfaction of personal needs which the market itself has created, and in an elitist lifestyle good enough to perplex and disorient one's self-dissatisfaction.

In a way, that is all that we can do. The triumph of the market economy has forced us back into our daily realities, and the daily realities are divorced from poetry and singing thoughts. As we learn from our early years, we cannot swim against the tide – no mention of it is made in the book *Time and How to Survive It* by Dr Med. I. Ocre. The world, riding, Milan Kundera said, on 'a wave of ugliness, visual, olfactory and gustatory', respects not intentions, but results. It is interested not in the meaning of things but in their use, and finds merit not in purpose but in what American pragmatist philosopher William James called the 'cash value' of the idea. Practical men and women, esteemed members of the 'me' generation, all those of us who, as Ezra Pound said, 'see *to kalon* decreed in the market place', would never cross the lines demarcated by these realities and look for meaning outside their periphery.

Content with ordinary certainties, uninterested in remote enquiries, and unwilling to question the breed of our expectations, we get excited talking about careers, au pairs and mortgages. As in the world of Flaubert's novels, a world in which all values are eroded and all dreams deflated, getting through in life seems to require an aggressive commitment to banality. Sometimes we feel irritated about things and need a few pints of perseverance to steady ourselves. I certainly did when I started using the service on the North London Link again, resumed after a week's break for refurbishments, only to find myself confronted with its usual cancellations. Occasionally, the *angst*, the dread of the individual at the disintegration of meaning, the irrationality that governs our lives in the very name of Reason, the spiritual and emotional void, the lack of purpose and the marginalisation of man by his own creations, systems and machines, hit us in the face. Unfortunately, however, we all know that we have to live with it. Even in California people cannot pass on their anguish to others. Capitalism has not as yet found the way we can pay others to feel for us.

We also know only too well the limits of our possibilities and the boundaries of our dreams. In the very last analysis, we can console ourselves things are not all that bad even if we do not do as well as we would like. After all, we are still doing better than

Shakespeare, who had only three horses, Mozart, who never had the chance to watch the World Cup on television, or El Greco, who had not even heard of Marks & Spencer's 'sexy sushi', which he probably could not have afforded as he was always involved in disputes over payments. Therefore, sensibly and happily, we fill our heads with practical dreams and our hearts with joy at all the things money can buy in what John Updike, the American novelist, called the 'boulevards of superfluity'. We plant our seeds in the field of rudimentalities – perhaps in a training course to perfect our smile or expansive outlook towards which executives may gravitate, a new designer kitchen or a 'new me' through cosmetic surgery, or, perhaps, a brain operation.

Living in the hotel of the world, there is not much else we can do apparently apart from enjoying all its passive distractions, the small gratifications without which life would look like hell, offered with the management's compliments. These small pleasures become a necessity from which it is almost impossible to escape, provide some amusement denied by everything but our acquired dislikes, and envelop us in a passion, in the absence of anything else, for the ordinary and the inconsequential. Not to delight in this madness, the lubricant of our pedestrian routines, would, indeed, be crazy.

Alternatively, we can resort to life or performance enhancing drugs, a practice, however, which is not very safe for, as the Stasi agent, the hero of a Thomas Brussig story, discovered, his genitalia expanded as a result to awesome proportions. Putting the trivial, Liz Hurley's knickers, into the focus of our sophisticated unconcern about anything of value would really look a much safer bet. With the devotion of a simpleton one can, of course, equally well seek salvation in some kind of religious fundamentalism or withdraw into the world of spirituality with a book of Lao Tzu under the pillow. The latter practice is nevertheless not as safe as it looks either. As Gabriel García Márquez tells us, Bolivar was believed to be 'dying in Guayaquil and later in Quito, of a gastric fever whose most alarming symptoms were lack of interest in the world and absolute spiritual calm.'

The fact that something has in the process been lost, died, is not even being taken seriously – there is no circumstantial evidence to prove it, for no body has been found. The great majority, self-satisfied with its terrestriality, carries on in a Kafkaesque society without any particular end in mind. Caring about the great goals of humanity, the individual's instinctual aims, the longings of the human spirit and the dreams of a life that makes sense, is the prerogative of the few, those viewed by the majority like the French poet's man who put his cap in the cage and went out, instead, with the bird on his head. Like the old sailor who, Ritsos tells us, 'spat at his feet and walked away to the small woods to piss', we have become too cynical to be concerned about anything.

The vision of the capitalist eternity, an *imperium sine fine* or an epoch at least as long as a geological period, even if as true as all our hopes and half of our fears, is as thrilling as vicarious sex. The end of history, Francis Fukuyama did not fail to notice, 'will be a very sad time'. The worldwide 'ideological struggle that called forth daring, courage, imagination and idealism, will be replaced', he said, 'by economic calculation, the endless solving of technical problems, environmental concerns, and satisfaction of sophisticated consumer demands. In the post-historical period and the edge of tomorrow, there will be neither art nor philosophy, just the perpetual caretaking of the museum of the human spirit' – which we may not even be able to locate in the terrifying void of the intergalactic capitalist space.

Though nonplussed and uncertain, we will, however, always be free to develop an interest in 'alternative lifestyles': swallowing tapeworms to stay in shape, piercing the willy or embracing Deepak Chopra's spiritual consumerism.

Part II: The System

1. The Teasing of Vesuvius

Not in the distant past, when it still took two to dance, the daily newspaper fitted in the inside pocket of a man's jacket, and 'out to lunch' had not yet turned into a profession, we believed that the future was ours. Indeed, we looked forward to it. Now we suspect it as people in the jungle suspect a deadly snake in every bush, mistrust its inability to look us straight in the face, fear it and pray against a 'third world of things too animated to be called mechanical, but too mechanical to be called alive'. The future, always pregnant and never delivering, cannot be called 'great' by right. It does not glide like a swallow across our longings. Disquietedly, science-fiction writer Ray Bradbury stopped, he said, trying to predict it, and instead, he tries 'to prevent it'.

Science and technology – genetics, nanotechnology, robotics or artificial intelligence, all of them, we are assured, celestially innocent as the moonlight – give us, presumably, the guarantee of progress we need. Nanotechnology, the science of small things, author Ray Kurzweil said, will enable us 'to redesign and rebuild, molecule by molecule, our bodies and brains and the world with which we interact, going far beyond the limitations of biology' – and past constraints; and decoding the 'book of life', the chemical letters of the genome, will enable the medical profession to diagnose and treat many incurable diseases with precision. The profound and disruptive transformation of life one can only expect will be crowned when genetics will be able to produce the super-race. Later on, and if the Trade Unions do not object, we may also gain immortality, munificently granted by Zeus to Tithonus, who had, however, regretfully forgotten to ask also for perpetual youth.

Closer to quotidianeity, mobile phones will be able to control and monitor heating and electricity, fingerprints will lock and unlock doors, refrigerators will order groceries, and smart toilets will perform health checks. The smart home, with a budget for its own upkeep, will be able to see, feel and react, make us tea, find lost keys or alert the emergency services. Alarm clocks, electric blankets, mixers and coffee makers will be able to talk to each other, and digital portraits will monitor the elderly so that we, happily, will not have to take care of them in person. In the meantime, the electronic means of surveillance, already allowing users to monitor homes remotely or to serve as armed border guards with a 500-metre range and a 'shoot-to-kill' policy, will make completely sure that every detail of our life, even our most private moments, can be policed by anyone in possession of the right equipment. 'Once you develop robots for urban warfare', professor Noel Sharkey, a senior fellow on the engineering and sciences research council, said, 'you can then start to use them for policing. We could police people at home.'

All this will, presumably, increase our freedom by expanding our control of everything. But, equally well, it may just mean fast lanes to hell. Bill Joy, the leading software innovator, was sure of it when he said that we are on the cusp of the perfection of an extreme evil beyond anything we ever knew. Science and technology, he warned, controlled by a few terribly empowered individuals, are working for 'the further perfection of extreme evil', at least as fearsome as nuclear, chemical and biological weapons. Computers, he predicted, a million times more powerful in twenty-five years time than today, will place technology beyond man's power to control; and robots, able to replicate themselves and possibly exceeding humans in intelligence, may well create havoc. Technology, Canadian media guru Marshall McLuhan said as far back as 1964, has reduced us to the 'sex organs of the machine world'. Little in the power of science and technology seems to convey much benevolence. The heroic model of science is now deeply flawed, and any breakthrough is, indeed, associated with new dangers – the greater the breakthrough, the greater the dangers.

Radioactive nuclear waste remains toxic for up to 300,000 years, but nobody, including those who plan more nuclear plants, knows how to handle it. Almost as bad might well be genetically engineered pathogens and genetically modified crops. Without any benefits for consumers or the Third World, both of which are supposed to be the prime beneficiaries, they threaten to contaminate non-GM crops and organic farming, as well as biodiversity. In the absence of long-term research into their impact, they may even constitute a threat to human health. Claims about benefits without 'collateral damage', which science promises to bring to mankind, seem to qualify for the book of cruel jokes to be reopened when we need to invent our last smile. For, as Vladimir Mayakovsky reminded us: when 'they teased Vesuvius, Pompeii perished.'

Man simply cannot be trusted with so much power, which in the name of development and economic growth, i.e. wealth and power, he is bound to misuse and abuse with catastrophic consequences. Combining the power of a giant with the wisdom of a simpleton can only turn life into a lived-in nightmare.

The 'land beyond all known lands and corners of the ideal', to use a Nietzschean expression, may well thus, be a fully dehumanised world controlled by computers, subject to nuclear disasters, deforestation and desertification of the environment, overpopulation, shanty towns, less personal security, greater social inequality, urban chaos, and wars over resources, particularly water. Next to all these dangers, which someone cheekily said, appeared only after women got the vote, stand the destruction of civilisations, hi-tech dictatorships, terrorism measuring eight and over on the Richter scale, financial crises that may throw the world into a deadly turmoil, or uncontrolled and brutal power in the hands of a power élite.

Futurologists working with leading companies to identify consumer trends do not give a very different picture. Oxygen bars where gasping customers are served pure oxygen all across Oxford Street will, they predict, become commonplace; a class of technological have-nots, filled with rage and frustration, will turn into the new threat to social stability; and the increasingly beleaguered middle class will be trapped in high-security ghettos with only their tamagotchi, robotic pets, for company. Susan Greenfield in her *Tomorrow's People* gives us another option: the splitting of the human race into two species, the 'enriched' in the developed countries and the 'naturals' in the developing world. The difference between them is bound to be, Lee Silver said in his *Remaking Eden*, the difference between humans and chimpanzees. The élite, Silver says, will be members of the GenRich class, the abilities of which even the most talented and gifted Natural-humans would be totally unable to match.

Even Wells, Verne, Huxley and Asimov did not predict such a gruesome and yet so distinct possibility. Genetic engineering, often associated with a rerun of racist eugenics experiments, could well be just 'a jumbo jet with bicycle brakes', Aeolus' bag of winds. The latter, opened by science's crew, can create havoc in our century which, in retrospect, we may one day regret having so enthusiastically welcomed.

What we think of the future is given to us by science fiction in its apocalyptic visions of a nightmarish world, dehumanised, programmed by computers, drugged and controlled by a power élite through robots, cloned armies, thought factories and mind-policing. Intelligence, memory, feelings and dreams are software, decoupled from the individual and eerily transformed into existential spare parts, playthings used by metahumans feeding on genetically 'enhanced' food. The new super-race, rather than enjoying its privileges, is living in sanitised underground quarters with the wretched masses, disavowed by fate, crowding the coprolalic, sordid, murderous streets of the New Era.

Science fiction is perhaps the most politically engaged of all literary genres, and Hollywood, capitalising on fascinating stories, does of course produce what sells. But, despite its spurious assumptions, behind its nightmarish vision of a future seeded with our inexorable efforts to improve 'God's creation' there is some artistic intuition which philosophy, politics or science lack, and which is in line with the subconscious, anonymous fears of the common man. The same intuition forced novelist Günter Grass' hand to write about the new department opened by his local museum in which 'our aborted children, pale, serious embryos, sit there in plain glass jars and worry about their parents' future'.

If only a small part of them were to come true in twenty-five years time, and provided that a future US president does not pre-emptively launch the Third World War, the war which will eradicate all wars, in preparation for what president George W. Bush, in his strange verbal stumblings, called 'time for the human race to enter the solar system', people may well be looking back for inspiration from our age. Yet, lethargically, our era was only too happy to believe, albeit only in the last ten years of the twentieth century, that all fundamental conflicts which have tormented humanity since the first angry word was ever uttered, are all things of the past. The belief, incredible as it was, is as reassuring as the pill the grandmother of the story took because she did not want more grandchildren. Perhaps someone will pray for us – for free if possible.

Progress is not as bad by definition as the *News of the World*'s moral crusades or spelling in what Salman Rushdie called the 'mighty democracy of mispronunciation, the United States'. And in spite of my bemoaning it, I neither could nor would look forward to settling back in times gone by.

Arcadia, the land of pastoral poetry and bucolic charm in Roman literature and later in that of the Renaissance, in which as it happens my family has its roots, does not have a place in my fantasies. Drinking the crystal clear fountain water of its mountains and listening to Daphnis' poetry does not really compensate for the time spent milking the goats. Nor do my own early experiences associated with the very long war years, 'years poorly spent' as Guillaume Apollinaire, the French poet, would have said, evoke any great desire to return to the past. The past, even if we can improve it, is for me associated with death and its defiance, poverty which ensured my clothes were never my size – 'you'll grow into them, don't worry!' and survival on grains of hope. And then when the '50s and, together with them, peace came, there were those insipid school days, dead as dried wood, and the victorious ultranationalist side's malodorous patriotism, considered natural as breathing and uplifting as drugs though far less expensive.

Peace and the progress that came with it made life so much easier. Just electricity, which now seems to be almost as old as New Labour, enables me to see at night, use my computer, listen to the radio, easily make a cup of coffee, safely store my food in the refrigerator or play music on a keyboard. It has also enriched my vocabulary. 'Feedback', a word coined by Norbert Weiner in 1948 to describe 'the use of controlling signals to modify the output, or behaviour of a machine or organism so that it will reach its goal', is now, in a time that technology has pervaded our thinking, a word I would occasionally use to describe my interaction with humans. Terrific scientific achievements have, meanwhile, transformed life on earth.

As Carl Sagan, a scientist whose reputation has fared better than science itself, reminds us, Queen Anne, pregnant eighteen times in the last seventeen years of the seventeenth century, had only five of her children born alive, and of them only one survived infancy only to die before reaching adulthood. Although the mortality rate remains the same – on average one death per person, as the Andorran actuary said – today children have a much better chance of survival. So do the adults protected against bubonic plague, which in the fourteenth century killed about a third of the population of the known world, and cholera, smallpox, diphtheria or the influenza, which after the First World War killed more people than the war itself. People are expected to reach the age of eighty rather than fifty which was the life expectancy in 1915; and the Earth can feed a hundred times more humans than it could in Christ's time.

On the other hand, of course, our world is enriched with new ailments – Aids, 'God's punishment on wickedness' as the American religious Right asserted, infertility, psychological disorders, chronic fatigue syndrome, Sars, asthma and ulcers, heart failures, the new variant of Creutzfeldt Jacob Disease, MRSA, C.diff and other conditions we are not even sure how to spell. The latest among them to be highlighted is obesity, a disease that has hit the West following the Americanisation of the food supply and the 'toxic environment' this has created. The notion of natural causes of death also needs to expand to include loss of life in acts of terrorism, air disasters, car accidents, inner city crime, man-made calamities – Chernobyl, Exon Valdez, Bhopal, all inexorable elements of our contemporary decoration. One might also note the loss of immunological fitness of commercially-bred animals and the reduced genetic diversity of various wild animal populations (wolves, cheetahs, seals) that leads to disease susceptibility.

Regardless of its benefits, progress also often makes life more difficult in some respects as, just to keep our head above water, we have to keep learning new things. Just when I managed to find my way around the room of an ultra modern hotel, in came high technology which, it seems to me, requires the training of an F-18 pilot; and just as I learnt how to handle the InDesign 2.0 in came the blogs.

Progress, and this is its fundamental feature that makes the whole difference, is underpinned by one principle only: the prospect of profit, as fierce in its love for life as the fire for the warehouse. Capitalism will never invest in anything unless the investors anticipate good returns on their investment. Nothing will ever be produced for a market without purchasing power, and this includes the digital revolution which, rather than lessen, has aggravated the world's divides between the poor and the rich. 'The free market', Freeman Dyson, the American physicist and futurologist, said in his *Imagined Worlds*, 'will not by itself produce technology friendly to the poor.'

Despairing, E.F. Schumacher, the German economist, conservationist and author of *Small is Beautiful*, noted: 'Call a thing immoral or ugly, soul-destroying or a degradation of man, a peril to the peace of the world or to the wellbeing of future generations: as long as you have not shown it to be "uneconomic" you have not really questioned its right to exist, grow and prosper.' This tendency, along with globalisation, are the strange-looking neighbours of the bovine details of our life, for whose appearance, Robert Graves, the English poet and novelist, might say once again, 'even in city parks excuses must be made to casual passers-by'. Every step forward looks, to quote Greek poet Engonopoulos, 'as if it is written on the other side of death announcements', like the time when death announcements were pinned on the neighbourhoods' electricity poles.

Riding on a wave of destruction, progress, which has not managed as yet to find a cure for the common cold, malignant and unsavoury, has, indeed, endangered our survival. To survive it, we need protection against progress itself and the forces behind it, the voracious free market and our insatiable appetite for more. Development, which is what progress is about, is destroying both our present and our future. Yet there are voices which insist that the process can be reversed without sacrificing any of our present comforts. Most unwilling to make changes is the US which, though inhabited by five per cent of the planet's population, uses one third of its resources. Virtue, the possession of which makes the poor proud, is a luxury the rich cannot afford.

To recall T.S. Eliot again, 'pray for those who choose and oppose.

2. A Fairy Tale

Science itself, 'value free' unless we are talking about research grants which are highly valued, is held to be neither moral nor immoral. Yet it offers, as Ludwig Wittgenstein said, no protection at the human level against the atrocities in which it played a part, as in the Holocaust, Hiroshima, Nagasaki and Dresden. Since Hiroshima its progress can no longer be seen as going hand-in-hand with the progress of humanity. Wittgenstein denounced 'pure science' as a 'cult' to which atomic physics, by claiming an ethical neutrality, has only contributed new pseudo-scientific myths. Paul Feyerabend, the Austrian-born philosopher of science who in his youth considered joining the SS for 'aesthetic reasons', scornfully dismissed, likewise, the idea that natural science contains knowledge independent of ideology or social prejudice. Claims to the contrary, he said, are a 'fairy tale'.

Science and technology, far from being neutral, are themselves ideological, encoded with values, transmitters of culture in the service of the system that employs them. Procrustes in modern dress, the nuclear scientist, Aldous Huxley said, will prepare the bed on which mankind must lie; and if mankind does not fit – well, that will be just too bad for mankind. Encoded with values, both science and technology transmit cultural assumptions and help to foster domination through an improved chain of control. The notion that scientific and technological power is *our* power is as fallacious as the idea that we are in control of it; it is a deadly illusion. The struggle of the oppressed, Herbert Marcuse melancholically stated, has ended in establishing a new, 'better' system of domination.

This 'better system' is not even subject to any public control. Genetic engineering has not been sanctioned by any Parliament and it does not seem to seek anybody's approval. But even if it were to accept public controls, democracy could not and would not function unless discussion and opinion were free from manipulation and domination. But, tactfully, like all those 'truth-loving Persians', who as Robert Graves noted 'do not dwell upon the trivial skirmish fought near Marathon', we prefer not to attach undue importance to such hapless specificities.

Scientists, the knights of progress, free spirits when they staged their revolution against the tyranny of medieval unreason, ended up servants of the system they had heavily contributed to create.

Propelled and ruthlessly exploited by hegemony-seeking interests, caught in situations demanding bravery rarely shown they have their share of responsibility for the ravages of time. On judgment day, when they will be called to explain why they took us down Nemesis Avenue, nobody will be prepared to listen to excuses of the kind: 'I was only doing my job' or 'those were my orders.' They cannot claim that their only interest was science itself. Rather than children picking up shells beside the great and unexplored ocean of truth, as Isaac Newton romantically saw himself, scientists are mercenaries in the corporate war against nature and humans.

Ozone depletion and global warming, air and water pollution, acid rain or the poisoning of the earth with toxic and radioactive waste could not have come without scientists' active involvement in the interests of the multinationals. Biotechnological research to standardise fruits, vegetables and now animals, is big business expected to bring good corporate profits. So is cloning, the scientific 'breakthrough', which will possibly end up by standardising humans too and made the world shiver and run for a megadose of tranquillisers.

Building the Titanics of the future seems not to worry scientists. Unlike Democritus, who 'would rather discover a single causal explanation than become king of the Persians', they would rather be kings. Plutarch, talking about Archimedes, the greatest scientist of antiquity, wrote he was 'such a lofty spirit that he never condescended to write any treatise on the manner of constructing all these engines of war. And as he held that this science of inventing and putting together engines ... to be vile and mercenary, he spent his talents and his studious hours in writing only of those things whose beauty and subtlety had in them no admixture of necessity.' Though incomprehensible in today's conditions, life itself was for him more important than science and all things associated with it – profits and power.

The scientists' involvement with the military, though it likes to keep its face indoors, is as cataclysmic. Indeed, the practical importance of science and technology was first recognised in connection with war – Galileo and Leonardo obtained government employment by their claim to improve artillery and the art of fortification. This is still the case as roughly half of the world's scientists are engaged in research work for the military, at least part-time, to improve the destructive capabilities of the existing technological wizardry. The development of the latter is such that future wars, even limited regional wars, are expected to be carried out at such a blindingly fast pace that nobody, not even the political leaders, much less the public, will be able to exert any control over their conduct. The baron of Montrognon is said to have killed six hundred Saracens who happened to get in his way as he was going to dinner. Science and technology, with noxious efficacy, do better – they can kill millions and much faster.

A metaphor for greed, science and technology are not by definition a force of progress. Neither of them is committed to anything but money. Trawlers using sonar and radar to detect shoals of fish – even small and far away shoals – scoop up vast quantities in high-tech nets. This may be a huge step forward for the fishing industry, but it does no favours to the environment and our future. Likewise, transplanting pig organs to humans may be helpful, provided the xenotransplants do not spread viral diseases from pigs to the human race. The drive behind the effort, which has not succeeded, was not, however, concern for our wellbeing but money – the market for pig organs could have been worth $7bn a year. The same is the case with ANDi, the genetically modified monkey created, we are told, to help research into the elimination of human diseases such as Alzheimer's and Aids.

Decoding the genes in the human body, unravelling the human blueprint, mankind's operating instructions, will give 'us', we are likewise assured, 'control over the next page of history'. The breakthrough is not complete as yet, for the genes' complicated functions and interactions are not yet understood. But, when completed, the process will transform medicine, enabling doctors to do what clinical trials have failed to achieve so far: diagnose and treat disease with drugs tailored precisely to the patient's genetic make-up. It will also help the food industry to carry on with intensive factory farming adjusted both to our genetic make-up, modified to resist listeria, salmonella, BSE, E.Coli, ISA in salmon and other awful things named with new letter combinations, and to the requirements of profitability. As the British Medical Association warned, genetics will further help the creation of new biological weapons, based on human genetic variability, to target particular ethnic groups. Other possibilities here include the production of genetically engineered anthrax, bioregulators that attack the immune and nervous systems or viruses such as that which recreates the 1918 'Spanish flu'.

At the same time, it is almost inconceivable that genetic experiments will not inaugurate a new race, the eugenic race, with the rich and powerful in the forefront right from the start. The reassurance offered by the British government that it will not allow genetic modification of embryos for reproductive purposes, i.e., that the path to GM babies will remain closed, is as hollow as its victory in Iraq. Once the road has been opened, the production of designer babies, who can grow up to be, for example, designer athletes, who, the Swedish-based academic Torbjorn Tännsjö said might already be a reality, is only a matter of time.

Despite its advantages, even the Internet, the oneiric technology, which US Vice President Al Gore, the 'father of the internet' as he has reputedly boasted, assured us in his time, 'will bring economic progress, strong democracies, better environmental management ... and a greater sense of shared stewardship of our small planet' is somehow of questionable value. A life in which all our connections with the world, from shopping to banking, entertainment, working or making friends, are done by cables looping past our front doors, can, however, reasonably enough be perceived as a threat rather than a promise. As newspaper columnist Michael Prowse put it, 'nothing could be further removed from the face-to-face physical being together of the Greek polis than atomistic screen-based interaction.' A virtual community, depriving people of their social identities, cannot replace the face-to-face interaction on which trust is built. Fortifying their isolation, it cheats them out of their human experiences.

Clifford Stoll, America's most famous computer sleuth, articulated the new problems stingingly early enough, in the mid-nineties. The Internet, he said, is 'a fantastic solution to a problem that does not exist..., (for) I have never met anyone standing at the street corner saying I need more information.' Readily accessible information in volumes nobody can digest, more often than not totally useless, and as a rule far beyond the expectations or even the desires of any normal person, does not make us any smarter. Besides, the Net is not the fountain of truth. Flooded with junk or second rate information, it has the capacity to crowd out thought and blur even further the difference between information and useful knowledge and between mechanised search procedures and traditional analysis. Voicing his fears, telecomputing, Stoll predicted, will seduce the next generation into a world of unreality and illusion, take it into 'a truly insubstantial universe', 'empty and heartless', arid, unsatisfying, divorced from human contact. Dumbfounded, Costas Cariotakis, the great Greek poet who 'died of disgust' at the age of 32, confessed: 'I haven't the slightest idea why this summer has come.' The same could be said about many of science's advances – progress itself.

The presumed freedom the E-topia gives us to find out the 'facts' for ourselves is quite limited; and the 'facts' on the Internet's advertorials, a potent mix of informative material and paid-for product placement that can convert into quick sales, are rather dubious. The new 'freedom', already commodified and vulgarised, is further undermined by the plagues and scourges of online life – the spam, the viruses, the false identities often used in networking sites catering in particular for young people, the deception, depravity and stupidity often associated with its contents. The online crime including identify theft, 'phishing', which is the duping of customers into revealing their personal information to criminals who can then access their bank accounts, 'pharming', which is the insertion of a bug on to the victim's computer that routes him to a bogus website when he requests his bank's website, have other and pretty painful consequences. Criminal gangs, mostly based in Eastern Europe, are already invading our personal world. Computers can be controlled externally by hackers through some of the most sophisticated types of crimeware and used for a variety of purposes. Credit card details are appropriated and sold for a few dollars. Passwords are stolen.

The same online 'freedom' is further its veritable denial the moment it makes possible the invasion of our privacy through the 'web bug' planted by some big business on our computers to track our movements online in embarrassing detail and then to target us with personalised advertising. This is a practice which also gives the intelligence agencies all the information they need about our web surfing habits. The age of electronic surveillance, which had already dawned before September 11, is now fully blossoming, making sure that even our emails to our children are being monitored. The time when the security services will be given sweeping powers to intercept emails and monitor traffic on the internet, find out which websites users look at, which pages they download, and which chatrooms or discussion groups they frequent, the day, in other words, that our privacy will be nationalised, may not be that far away.

This is the reason the EU has reacted so strongly to Google's intention to organise our personal lives – our choices, lifestyles and thoughts relating to anything from careers, partners and leisure to investment, religious practices and sexual preferences – by scanning our private e-mails to locate the key words that generate the personalised ads that will meet our needs. Such filling of millions of people is the totalitarian state's dream.

The public sphere which, it is claimed, the Internet has made available to the citizens of the world is also of questionable value. The opportunities are open to privileged groups only – white, educated, well off and English speaking, mostly Americans. They set the agenda in most areas of public discussion in a way which reflects their own concerns, dominates its mode and conduct, and influences the choices society makes as no other groups can. This is the reason, perhaps, that Internet censorship is spreading so rapidly – it is practised now by about two dozen countries. On the other hand, though an open medium, the web cannot deliver the egalitarianism it has promised. True, anyone can text his thoughts to Twittervision, contribute to Wikipedia or publish a photo of his mother-in-law on Flickr, but very few do. Web 2.0 is, indeed, dominated by an èlite that represents less than two per cent of registered users. But even so, and although they do not have access to power which is vital in getting the facts right, bloggers can be quite useful in a media world dominated by corporations.

Postmodernism, embodying Jean François Lyotard's 'incredulity toward metanarratives', has dismissed science altogether. It is nothing more, it asserts, than a 'narration', a 'myth' or a social construct. Its discourse about reality is just as good as any other including the religious, the mythical or the superstitious discourses, as if all the latter could offer another paradigm which explains the orbits of the planets better than science. For the postmodernists there are no facts, just interpretations relating to particular circumstances as a woman in Trinidad was happy to verify for my benefit. When I asked her how many square feet there are in an acre, she, in turn, asked me back 'where?'

Questioning science, the postmodernists have questioned progress – 'progress towards perfection' according to Darwin's comforting doctrine of evolution. Sceptical about the universality of all the great 'scientific' theories, they have also attacked knowledge itself as deeply political. Knowledge, Nietzsche, followed by Heidegger, said, is an invention that masks the will to power, the disciplining of people and their domination. Foucault denounced the claims of science and technology regarding truth and objectivity as part of an intellectual economy in which paucity and manipulation characterise truth-seeking, and Heidegger attacked science for assaulting nature. The 'technological frenzy' of modern man, the latter said, treats nature and human beings only in terms of pure manipulation which manifests the 'spiritual decline' of the West. For Heidegger, 'agriculture is today a motorised food industry, in essence the same as the manufacture of corpses in gas chambers and extermination camps, the same as the blockage and starvation of countries, the same as the manufacture of atomic bombs.'

The tone of the discourse which questions science as the bearer of truth was set by Karl Popper. His notion of falsifiability rested on the assumption that a theory is good only if its empirical predictions are not contradicted by subsequent observations or experiments. This is the 'empiricist dogma', which expects the impossible, i.e. the testing of an infinite range of scientific hypotheses each one of which can create an exponentially increasing range of further hypothetical variables. The impossibility of doing so fuelled the contemporary radical scepticism which denied science's reliability altogether as if knowledge had not advanced dramatically since the sixteenth century. Science, scepticism holds, is not knowledge but faith.

American philosopher of science Thomas Kuhn, in his *The Structure of Scientific Revolutions*, the most influential book in modern philosophy of science, argued further that science proceeds by imaginative leaps and bounds from one 'paradigm' to another. Each paradigm, i.e. the problems under scrutiny, their theoretical framework and the experimental procedures for their solution, is nevertheless unable to accommodate discrepancies and anomalies. It is, thus, succeeded by yet another theory or set of beliefs. What Kuhn objected to are the non-scientific considerations or the non-empirical factors which result in changes of paradigm which, once accepted, take scientists once again down the wrong road.

Paul Feyerabend went a step further when he described science as a 'particular superstition'. The 'similarities between science and myth' he said in his book *Against Method*, 'are indeed astonishing.' For him, all methodologies have their limitations, and the only 'rule' that survives is 'anything goes' within 'rules and standards' which he nevertheless did not define. In 1992, two years before he died, Feyerabend did, however, distance himself from the anti-scientific attitudes of 'relativists of all sorts', the 'fly-by-night mystics' and 'prophets of a New Age'.

Science and technology cannot, however, be dismissed as a myth, a superstition; and they are not good or bad by definition. Like Mozart's Magic Flute, they can, if purified, inspire love, and, if not, lust. As Raymond Williams observed, science is at worst neutral. It provides, Pythagoras said before him, the means both of man's liberation and destruction. Hence the latter's insistence that only those purified in body and spirit should be entrusted with its secrets. His views, embalmed and exhibited in the glass-window of the academy for the benefit of his epigons, did not make all that much difference. Abstracted from a whole way of life, science is dangerous; and in the hands of the 'unpurified', the industrial-military complex, it is ever-ready, as Primo Levi, the Italian poet, put it, to 'extend the desert into the Amazon forests, into the living heart of our cities, into our very hearts'.

The question, therefore, is whether science and technology will be allowed to carry on distorting our nature and essence, whether the existing mode of being will be accepted as the only mode of being. Heidegger's answer was 'yes' to the unavoidable use of technological objects, but 'no' to their claim of exclusively owning us. Still, science and technology, rather than being our destiny, seem to be our fate, Damocles' sword suspended by a hair over our heads.

The problem is not progress itself. It is, instead, the forces in charge of it, the heinous forces of greed, and also the very high price the individual, society and the planet pay for it. In a simple form, this is the price the inhabitants of the small Greek island of Skyros paid when in the nineteenth century West Europeans offered, and the islanders happily accepted, cheap imports of manufactured rubbish in exchange for the treasures with which the millenniums had endowed the island. Disempowered by what Nietzsche called the 'wisdom of superficiality', enriched by the material benefits accrued in the process, and slaves to a way of thinking from which it is extraordinarily difficult to detach ourselves, we do just the same.

Progress, intoxicated by the sound of its own pharyngeal voice, has arrogantly turned into our master, throwing the whole of our existence into a state of crisis. The crisis is not just social, environmental, institutional, personal or cultural. It is primarily a spiritual crisis which has paralysed the will and left us abandoned to the four winds. But, meanwhile, Merry Lane, with plenty of lawnmowers, has run out of grass. Eugène Ionesco, the playwright, terrified at the ever 'victorious' march of history, appealed to the 'progressive' spirits of this world not to improve the lot of mankind, if they really wish it well.

He was not even heard in an age, our age, which, obsessed with control, is able to control everything but its own insane drive to control.

3. Ferocious Beasts

Eager to form a coalition against terror, the West has no intention of forming a similar coalition in the interests of Justice, the best shield against terrorism. It lacks, as poet Andreas Kalvos would say, 'the sweet serenity of the just'. In spite of the smouldering resentment at its policies, Justice, particularly for the Americans, relates only to getting bin Laden 'dead or alive'. The world's moral order on which just social, economic, political and cultural institutions can be built is beyond their concern, valueless as poetry and annoying as the flu. On the agenda, instead, is the consolidation of a market controlled by oligopolies, those monsters indulging in unnatural acts of capitalist greed, whose ever-tightening grip over the world economy is nothing less than frightening.

Trapped in the net of the global forces of capitalism, what

Mahathir Mohammad, Malaysia's former prime minister, called a 'jungle of ferocious beasts', producers and consumers have become the raw meat that feeds the few hundred top companies which control the global economic output. Just three companies, Barry Lynn, senior fellow at the America Foundation, stated, account for 75 per cent of global iron ore production, two companies, Nike and Adidas, have captured 60 per cent of the global trainer market, four companies in the UK account for 94 per cent of supermarket sales, just ten groups in the US account for half of all retail sales, with single companies often capturing more than 75 per cent of particular product markets, and so it goes on.

Oligopolistic tendencies are clear in several key areas – pharmaceuticals and healthcare, financial services and banking, software, defence and telecommunications, oil, car and airplane manufacturing, shipping, industrial components, entertainment and the media. In eight sectors of the economy just the top five corporations control fifty per cent of the global market in a way which enables them to dictate policies to world bodies, including the EU. Wal-Mart, the world's largest retailer, Charles Fishman says in his book *The Wal-Mart Effect*, is not even subject to market forces 'because it's creating them'. Imperceptibly, the world economy has turned into the hostage of the oligopolies with the consumer, their prisoner, safely kept behind tall walls. Kavafis, the poet, may well wonder again how this has happened as he 'never heard the noise or the sound of the builders'.

The immense power such corporations have accumulated since US president Ronald Reagan and British prime minister Margaret Thatcher opened the way to the unregulated market is evident in their vast fortunes. Just one of them, General Motors, has an annual revenue which matches the combined GDP of Ireland, New Zealand, Uruguay, Sri Lanka, Kenya, Namibia, Nicaragua and Chad. Though only 153rd in the 2006 league of the billion dollar brands, a long way after Exon Mobil, HSBC, IBM, Nestlé, Coca Cola, Boeing, Sony or Disney, McDonald's alone is financially stronger than the economies of Tanzania, Ethiopia and Sudan put together. And as nothing is good enough, they all still strive for more. Like Theodora, the wife of Byzantine Emperor Justinian, who regretted that 'God had not endowed her with more orifices to give more pleasure to more people at the same time', they keep looking for new openings.

The revolution capitalism is undergoing is also evident in the astonishing transformation of mid-20th century managerial capitalism into financial capitalism that has turned the globe into what economist Cornelius Castoriades has called 'a planetary casino' of currency and finance speculation. The speculative trader and arbitrageur has taken the place of the manager, and the financier that of the producer. The aim is to make money rather than things – capital is now a source of revenue that has left miles behind any income earned from labour. One implication of this new development is that the bonds that used to exist between employers and employees, owners and managers, and companies and their shareholders have loosened up to such an extent that nothing but cash seems to matter any longer.

Within the new structures a host of complex new financial products deriving from traditional bonds, equities, commodities and foreign exchange, the 'derivatives' of which options futures and swaps are the best known, has emerged with new players, notably the hedge funds and private equity funds, coming into play. This new financial capitalism, which remains as unregulated as capitalism was a century ago, is beyond the ability of most legislators even to understand and of any national government to handle.

Private equity funds, this 'dark energy' investing in assets not tradeable in the stock market and above any public control, is the most aggressive force in this new capitalist scenery. The monstrous power they have acquired is amply demonstrated by the sum of $3,861bn spent in 2006 on global mergers and acquisitions – their volume suffered a dramatic fall in the second half of 2007 and the early part of 2008 as credit dried up; but in 1995 their value was only $850bn.

The activities of the funds, justified in terms of benefits from economies of scale, larger balance sheets which enable them to take more risks, and more secure earnings due to diversification, are nevertheless questionable, for behind the drive for money and power lies a shaky underlying financial structure. Concerns have also been raised due to the secrecy that surrounds them, the range of the companies they own, the extremely large returns reaped for their partners, the politically sensitive deals they enter, their refusal to endorse any principles of responsible investment and the scandalous tax advantages they enjoy. Regarding the latter, Nicholas Ferguson, one of the top figures in the UK private buyout industry, breaking the sector's taboo on talking about tax, said executives 'pay less tax than a cleaning lady'.

Wielding power without responsibility, the private equity funds also stand accused by many others, including Trade Unions, for the disastrous effects their quick-profits policy has on the long-term viability of companies and on jobs, communities and the environment. Socialist MEPs have, likewise, denounced their 'investor-friendly' emphasis, which has turned them into a major threat to Europe's social achievements, while financial regulators see in them a systemic risk to the stability of the financial system. UK private equity funds are the second biggest buyers of overseas companies after the American ones.

This global leviathan system, supported by unregulated hedge funds, networked computer systems, advanced telecommunications, fast transportation systems for people, goods and services, and an incredible information processing capacity to manage its complexities, has eliminated physical distances. It has turned the entire world into its playground. Its colossalism, Theodore Roszak, the Californian ecopsychologist, wrote in the 80s, when the global had not yet triumphed over the local and the world was not yet at the oligopolies' mercy, 'the bigness of things ... of industrial cultures, world markets, financial networks, mass political organisations, public institutions, military establishments, cities, bureaucracies endangers the rights of the person and the rights of the planet.' Yet, no effective opposition to it can develop.

Reduced to an almost meaningless political and economic unit, and largely unable to control their development, the nation state is simply overwhelmed by the forces it helped to unleash. Indeed, the 'mega-institutions', protected by the libertarian version of truth, the absolute freedom from government control or inspection, which means not only free gun ownership, but also radical *laissez faire* economics, and consolidated further through mergers and acquisitions, are beyond the ability of anyone to control or even regulate. Rupert Murdoch, going on the offensive, even asserted at some point that regulations are, in effect, a reinvention of socialism. Corporate finance makes sure no official opposition to its power can develop without serious consequences – opposition emanates only from those inhabiting the land beyond the reach of money. The politicians with a voice, as Orwell would say, nearly as silent as a voice can be while still remaining a voice, have neither the guts nor the motivation to act; those investing in the stock market, often ordinary householders, prefer to shut their eyes and enjoy the benefits of their corporate investments in the form of rising share prices; and international institutions, the World Trade Organisation, the International Monetary Fund and the World Bank, are ever ready to offer protection to the multinationals if the going gets rough.

This was the case, when Canadian publishers complained that the vast resources at the disposal of, and economies of scale achieved by, US publications in Canada posed a threat to their survival and to Canadian culture in genera – the WTO backed the US publications. Canada's complaint was dismissed, for it used culture 'as a pretence for discriminating against imports'. The same violence is evident in the dealings of the IMF and the World Bank against impoverished countries, mainly in Africa. In one instance, the IMF forced the government of South Korea to guarantee the repayment of bad debts owed by private Korean banks to private foreign banks. The Korean people had to pay billions of dollars in taxes so that their foreign creditors could collect the money they had privately loaned.

The economic consequences of the unchallenged dominance of the oligopolies are far more dramatic than we dare to think. Producers of goods and components who depend on oligopolies for their survival, including all those to whom corporations outsource risky or unprofitable parts of their business, see their prices dictated and their margins squeezed. This strong arm policy, as practised by supermarkets, has been denounced by the farmers' union in the UK as unfair and unethical – in India large retailers, particularly foreign chains such as Carrefour, Wal-Mart and Tesco, are not even allowed to enter the market. Consistently pursued by corporations, expansion of the retail sector puts millions out of business while extreme outsourcing sets supplier against supplier, worker against worker, and nation against nation.

As disturbing is the power the corporations have acquired to manipulate prices in a way that is leading to extreme pricing distortions, their extreme profiteering as demonstrated in the profit figures released by energy companies or banks, or their failure to introduce new technologies in areas such as renewable energy or environmentally friendly practices. The free market is free for the conglomerates to enrich themselves, but not for the planet, which is ruthlessly exploited, the consumer who has to pay the cost of their outrageously high profits, or the labour force, even the American one, who fails to profit from the massive expansion of corporate profits. The 'invisible hand' of competition, which, Adam Smith predicted, would reduce excess business profits to normal levels, has turned out to be as good as a racing certainty.

Ordinary Americans, Lawrence Summers, president of Harvard University from 2001 to 2006 said, do not feel on the same boat as US corporations and their chief executives. Gains have been unequally distributed, real wages have failed to keep pace with productivity growth, and unskilled immigration has kept earnings down. The same warning was given by Ben Bernanke, chairman of the US Federal Reserve. Middle earnings, he said, rose by 11.5 per cent between 1979 and 2006, except that the earnings of those near the top rose by a third, and that of those near the bottom by just 4 per cent. Huge increases in the pay of top executives, Jean-Claude Trichet, president of the European Central Bank, also and rather tactfully, stated, 'are not understood by the people in our democracies'. Many, including nearly all the Democrats elected to Congress in 2006, believe that, as a result, the future livelihood, not only of labour, but also of the middle class is at risk. 'Corporate America', Lou Dobbs, CNN's star anchorman, expressing the US middle class' disillusionment with the corporations, said, 'has lost its conscience'. Hence the moderates' fear that the way the new capitalism works could easily fuel a political backlash against the free market itself.

This was certainly the case when an American investment bank, German financiers and a London-based hedge fund managed to sell their 'structured finance' deals to Greek state pension funds at highly inflated prices, in effect ripping them off to enrich themselves further at the pensioners' expense. The *Financial Times* opined that 'this is the seamy side of international finance that bankers do not usually like to talk about.' Yet, unsurprisingly, on the surface nothing in this corrupt deal seems to be exceptional except that the Greeks did not take kindly to it.

The political consequences of the corporations' unlimited power are as important. Governments, linked to multinationals so closely that they can take an aspirin for each other's headache, are no longer free to determine their course of action. This is so evidently the case with Rupert Murdoch's ever expanding media empire, which the British government has been forced to take a look at albeit in order to do absolutely nothing. As a result, the citizens lose their right to choose because this right is annulled the moment the decision-making process is taken over by the market. Identifying the danger, what Ernest Gellner, the social anthropologist called in 1994 'the tyranny of the market', Professor David Marquand, the British political thinker, stated bluntly in the mid-nineties, before the dominance of the oligopolies was so blatant: 'Globally and nationally, we shall sooner or later have to choose between the free market and the free society.' The identification of the all-too-powerful market with democracy in effect denies democracy itself.

Indeed, the civic society, fragmented and dysfunctional, structurally weak and ideologically disarmed, cannot stand up to the power of the mighty forces of capitalism – Monsanto, News Corporation, Nike, Wal–Mart, GlaxoSmithKline, Shell, Microsoft or McDonald's, all metaphors for a global economic system gone awry. Engaged in 'asymmetrical warfare', resistance groups may annoy the multinationals, but they cannot bring them to their knees. The power to shape what is common to us all, and therefore to each one of us, evaporated the moment the free market assumed full control of the realm. The system is so breathtakingly powerful and, in addition, our individualism so entrenched that there is really not all that much one can do about it. 'Powerless with a guitar' as Günter Grass put it rather melancholically, we can only watch life go by while, 'finely meshed and composed, power has its way'.

As the servant of big business, all governments can do is provide the technological infrastructure, human resources and what is euphemistically called a 'flexible market', which will stimulate multinational investment. Competing thereby for the goodwill of the wealthy, they antagonise their own nationals, whose allegiance is nevertheless bought by the promise of improved living standards through globally-induced economic growth. At the same time, increasingly dependent on corporations for solutions in all spheres of the public domain, they see their traditional policy-making structures constantly undermined, marginalised, even ridiculed. AOL's Gerald Levine reportedly articulated the point when he asserted that 'the global media is becoming more important than governments, than NGOs, than the educational institutions'

The marginalisation of governments by the multinationals is, however, now attracting some attention even in the UK. Britain's willingness to sell key industries to overseas business, the chief executive of Rolls-Royce stated in 2007, is turning the country into an 'aircraft carrier'. Decisions regarding investment and disinvestment will, as a result, be made 'in their national interest rather than Britain's'. Hence the hostility of Britain to the possibility of a Russian takeover of its gas industry, the hostile reaction of the US to the takeover of P&O by Dubai Ports World or the US Congress veto in 2005 of the bid by CNOOK, the Chinese oil group, for Unocal, the oil company. Hence also the hostile reaction of France, Luxembourg and Spain to the acquisition of Arselor, Europe's largest steelmaker, by Mittal Stell, the global company headed by Indian entrepreneur Lakshmi Mittal.

The same hostility to foreign takeovers is evident throughout Europe as 'the vast majority of member states', the European Commission stated, shows 'a strong reluctance to lift takeover barriers'. In a downbeat assessment, the Commission's conclusion was that most EU governments remain unconvinced by its own assertion that takeovers offer 'benefits for companies, investors and ultimately the European economy as a whole'.

Globalisation was initially opposed by the continental Left on the grounds that it erodes the economic, political and cultural autonomy of the nations of the world in favour of the Anglo-Saxon countries, principally the USA. Now, and as the balance of power is shifting from the West to the emerging nations of the South, it is also opposed by a rekindled Western nationalism engulfing countries most addicted to selfish calculation.

Open markets and free capital flows were the flag of the Anglo-Saxon at the time they were synonymous with the advance of western business into the developing world. Globalisation was not a problem either when outsourcing jobs and services to third world countries, and thereby reducing job opportunities in the West, was not a practical proposition, or when immigration from developing nations to the West had not assumed today's massive dimensions that keeps wages down and threatens the cohesion of the West.

Likewise, it was not a problem when liberalisation of trade meant new inroads into the economies of the developing world. But now, at a time when even on the small Greek island of Skyros there is a shop in the village square run by a Chinese couple who trade in China-made clothing, things are different. The framework of what I had taken as reality is broken. Globalisation is no longer what it used to be.

And the West does not like it, as it does not like what is called fair trade, if fair trade is to benefit all rather than just 'us'. Protectionism, it whinges like a poor tiger who had never tasted a Christian, guarantees only perpetual poverty. Coerced by the IMF, the World Trade Organisation and the World Bank rather than the intellectual merits of the argument, most of the poor countries have, thus, halved their import tariffs in the last twenty five years. As a result, the industrialised countries' products and services flood their markets unhindered. But the West, some gigabytes short of chivalry, has not reciprocated. Liberalisation of trade is for others, not itself. Even in the post-September 11 era, the WTO's ruling general council could not make any commitments to reduce the trade-distorting agricultural subsidies and high tariffs that act as a barrier against developing countries' exports in areas where they have a comparative advantage.

As a result, as Oxfam estimated, tariffs facing the exports of manufactured goods from poor countries are, on average, four times higher than goods travelling in the opposite direction. This costs the poor about $100bn a year which is three times the amount they receive annually in aid, and twice the amount promised to halve world poverty, cut infant mortality and provide universal primary education.

The hypocrisy of the West, its double standards, is highlighted by the protectionist agricultural policies of the EU, designed, incidentally, to support the richer northern European farms – 80 per cent of CAP's subsidies go towards supporting grain, beef and dairy as opposed to olive oil and wine which are predominantly grown in southern Europe. These policies are matched by those of the United States and Canada, South Korea and Japan. Subsidies offered to farmers of the developed world are, indeed, so large that almost 40% of the farm income in the member countries of the Organisation for Economic Cooperation and Development comes from government-mandated support. At the same time, the West's barriers to the import of goods from poor countries, particularly labour-intensive industrial goods and processed food, are so high that rich countries collect tariffs four times higher on their imports from those countries than on imports from other rich countries.

The developing countries can, thus, under no circumstances compete against the heavily subsidised agricultural produce of the developed countries or cope with the other import restrictions which, under the terms of the Uruguay Round, ought to have already been phased out. They just cannot export, and *Fairtrade*, endorsed even by Nestlé, one of the most disliked companies in the world and boycotted by ethical consumers, is not going to redress the fundamental injustices in the world's trade systems.

Cotton is just one example, the most emotive, that illustrates the hopelessness of the situation. Though West and Central African countries produce high-quality cotton at low cost, their farmers have been devastated by a big expansion of US cotton exports helped by $4bn a year in subsidies paid to US cotton farmers, which is three times the entire US aid budget for Africa. The willingness of the European Union to reduce its own cotton subsidies to Greece and Spain in order to reduce their trade-distorting effects did nothing to move the Americans. As they have made clear, they are just not prepared even to discuss the issue. Causing an outrage, they tried instead to persuade the Africans to diversify away from their dependence on cotton exports.

The Africans at the same time swim in a sea of suffering because the same Western subsidised goods, which make it impossible for them to export, are dumped on their own market. Yet just a 0.7% increase in exports from a developing country would generate as much income as such a country receives every year in aid.

Along with all this, the United States, alarmed because as president Bush said while still looking forward to making sense, 'more and more of our imports are coming from overseas', refuses to eliminate the lucrative $4bn a year tax break for large exporters that has been ruled illegal by the WTO, or lift the import restrictions on textiles, clothing and footwear. Likewise, it refuses to end its over-muscular approach and highly discriminatory controls of steel imports and moderate its overzealous use of anti-dumping policies directed against the exports of Third World countries. Anti-dumping policies, in particular, enacted for the benefit of domestic cartels, violate fundamental competition principles. As distasteful are the concealed and yet heavy export subsidies offered by the US government to American farmers, those growing crops such as corn, wheat, rice and soya beans, or the insistence of the developed world, particularly the US again, on gaining maximum benefit from trade-related intellectual property rights which determine access to medicines.

Meanwhile, the EU members and other developed countries continue to subsidise many corporations, including the car industry, and are invading the service sector of the developing world, including the latter's health services, by cream-skimming their resources. The pursued liberalisation, incidentally, precludes free movement of labour which would increase the world's income and benefit people in the poorer countries. It does not affect hostility to immigration or offshore outsourcing, both of which particularly trouble the US and question its commitment to globalisation. Nevertheless, despite all obstacles the West raises in blocking free trade if it works to its disadvantage, the system is cracking – Chinese trading in Skyros' village square was not a spectacle I expected to see in my lifetime.

Happy to collect the interest on loans made to Third World corrupt or repressive regimes, those on the receiving end of corporate bribes, the West at the same time does next to nothing under the

Heavily Indebted Poor Countries initiative to reduce their impossible debts. Despite the lip service it still pays to 'principles', it refuses, likewise, to honour the commitment made by all UN members, with the exception of the US, to a standard volume of official assistance. The donor countries, the OECD said in a 2007 report, have once again failed to honour the pledges made in Gleneagles in 2005 under the pressure of a crowd of one million people in London and many more in many other parts of the world – a failure which, incidentally, shows how much disrespect politicians have for their people. These pledges were subsequently watered down at the G8 summit in Germany's Heiligendamm.

Rather than increased, aid has thus shrunk with the result that most highly-indebted poor countries still spend more than ten per cent of their revenues on debt service – and this after receiving debt relief. The West, in the meantime, shamefully continues to tie aid, and also loans, to demands made to the Third World to create the conditions for 'more favourable business environments' and to 'open up' trade, while advancing programmes on the strength of political considerations, including co-operation against terrorism, as the latter is defined by the US.

Oxfam warned: 'the system is facing a crisis of legitimacy' generated by the 'blatant hypocrisy and double standards that govern the behaviour of rich countries towards poor countries'. But neoliberalism, like 'the wolf that comes down from the woods to look on the dead dog and to weep', as Nicos Gatsos, the joyfully melancholic poet, might say again, has no solutions to offer. The ratio of average US incomes to those in Sierra Leone, the country in which only the arms dealers wear shoes, is seventy to one, but it is not going to ameliorate. Following current trends, it will instead be at least one hundred and twenty to one by 2050. The free market fundamentalists' unswerving faith in the redeeming power of the market, Ulrich Beck, professor of sociology at the university of Munich stated, has proved to be a dangerous illusion. Adam Smith's folk version of economics, according to which an invisible hand will ensure that, if each person seeks to maximise his own wealth, the wealth of all will be maximised and everybody will be happy, has requested some more time to prove itself. What has turned out to be true, instead, is Marx's prediction that under capitalism inequality will grow as wages will decline – in relative, not absolute, terms.

The beneficiaries of globalisation are not the poor of the world, but the world's richest three hundred and eighty-five people, who have more wealth than the poorest forty-five percent of the entire population of the earth. The craftier people are, Aristotle has said, the more unjust they are. Nor are the First World's consumers and citizens the beneficiaries. It is the corporations. Only one per cent of those who participated in a survey conducted by the French newspaper *Le Monde* thought otherwise.

The entry into the world economy of large numbers of computer literate Asians armed with mobile phones has, of course, changed the picture dramatically in the space of only a few years. The expanding middle class in countries such as China, India, Russia or Brazil knows what to demand and often gets it. But 'rising inequalities', an Unctad report stated, 'are becoming more permanent features of the world economic landscape' which is what denies moral legitimacy to the new world order and turns it into a new world disorder. Globalisation has done nothing much to diminish the poverty of the many; and though the gap between richest and poorest is more extreme today than at any time since the start of the industrial revolution, income inequality within cities as well as between urban and rural areas and First and Third World countries, glittering wealth on the one hand, and harrowing poverty on the other, ugly, frightful and obscene, continues to increase fully denying all the professed values of our civilisation. Perhaps, as poet Pablo Neruda penned, God is the enemy of the poor human being.

Hence, fighting back, many non-western countries, including South Korea and Japan, try to block the further expansion of Anglo-Saxon capitalism to their countries. Others, like Thailand, are determined to reassert Thai control over multinationals and all those who are 'exploiting' Thailand's open door. These protectionist policies can easily gravitate towards extreme forms of nationalism, xenophobia and anti-modernism.

The future of both the Third World and the First World's poor seems to have been carved by destiny upon the darkness of the night. Those who benefited from the global economy – for example, the UK's one thousand richest individuals – look composed, relaxed and unworried while trying a bit of therapy to overcome their affluenza whose symptoms, I am told, include lack of meaning and purpose in life, shame, guilt and addictive or compulsive behaviour.

The rest, those who share their secrets with poverty, struggle just to survive. One third of them, all those who are forced by an invisible ceiling to keep their eyes on the ground, live in or on the margin of poverty; and one quarter are at or below the government's minimal level of income. By the end of 2000, 14.5m people in the UK – 26% of the population – were living in poverty. Of them, 9.5m could not afford to keep their homes adequately heated and damp-free, and 7.5m were too poor to engage in social activities such as visiting friends and family or attending weddings and funerals. In the meantime, children of poor parents are more likely than not to grow up poor themselves, which does not say all that much about the free market's equality of opportunity.

The US and the UK, the two countries which provide the free market model, both Unicef and the UN Development Programme, said, are the worst two industrial countries in which children grow up. Children do consistently much better in the countries with a social democratic or corporatist model of capitalism.

But as anger, 'the spring of all life's horror' as vengeful Medea pronounced, masters their resolve, the earth's disinherited may well opt for the unexpected. Terror seems, indeed, inevitable if, as Karen Armstrong, the historian, said, we ignore the plight of the Other. Naturally, raw violence, resorted to by those who have no B-52s, Apache helicopters equipped with Hellfire antitank missiles, or command and control systems that allow the tracking of everything on computer screens, will be decried by the West as 'evil'. The violence done with all the help high technology can offer is in accordance, presumably, with God's will and the requirements of civilisation.

Worried by the widespread unease, Alan Greenspan, former US Federal Reserve chairman, was forced, when talking in Wyoming, to acknowledge that these are not the assertions of the lunatic left, but of decent people who are bothered about 'the way markets distribute wealth and about the effects of raw competition on the civility of society'. As worried, James Wolfensohn, former president of the World Bank, deplored the developed world's lack of interest in global poverty – such an interest is 'near a low point', he said in 2004, while Kofi Annan, the ex-UN Secretary General, warned the multinationals earlier that they may face a backlash as global rules for protecting corporate interests have become far more robust than those safeguarding social standards.

The backlash did occur, with the growth of the anti-globalisation movement and the political, even governmental, opposition to corporate consolidation in a way reminiscent of the revolt against the 'robber barons', Rockefeller, Carnegie or Jay Gould a century ago. Although the Americans would dispute it, the backlash also occurred with the assault on America's focal symbols of financial and military power, caused by the despairing rage against the abuses of American power.

This rage is evident not just in so many Third World countries but also in many third world neighbourhoods of first world cities, in all places where, as Dante would say, 'pain is the host'. Yet the political consensus of the post-cold war era embracing free trade, deregulation and unfettered capitalism remains as solid as the Frankfurt Stock Exchange. Besides, as things have developed, the multinationals can neither survive only on their own home market nor can they deal with the new and tougher economic conditions which force them to expand ceaselessly and intensify their worldwide activities. In this, they have, of course, the full support of the US, the Power which, American diplomatic historian Gerald Haines said, has 'assumed, out of self-interest, responsibility for the welfare of the world capitalist system'.

The new world order, Michael Hardt and Toni Negri state in *Empire*, a book published in 2000, has set its paradigm: 'centralized construction of norms and far-reaching production of legitimacy.' The latter, pursued through military action under cover of universal values, was expected to lead to a peace imposed upon those economically exploited and politically repressed.

But the model lays now in tatters in the streets of the extremes. And yet, only too willing to turn subsequently its own cities into fortresses to protect itself against the rage of the disenfranchised, the West has no desire to do anything in the interests of fairness.

The current transformation of the world sees the centre of gravity shifting gradually to emerging new markets in a way bound to create a new multipolar system that will eventually challenge the dominance of the West. But not its values. Materialism, the ultimate instrument of globalisation that proffers the ephemera that the West holds dear, will make sure of it. But, meanwhile, the increasingly Asian economic and political flavour of globalisation is more likely than not to force the leading Western economic Powers to fall back upon the protectionism they so earnestly deplore.

Globalisation will then look very different to how it appears today, and that only if we are blessed with good fortune. If not, Panajotis Kondylis, a neo-Marxist close to the European New Right, said, a world of expanding population, limited resources, growing consumerism and spiritual stupor, can only expect devastating wars pursued for vital resources.

When this happens, we might acknowledge, like Euripides, that 'everything yields place to something else', and then, in the absence of any other useful option, get together in the wine bar to recall the good old days when war was just 'war on terror'.

4. A Cultural Bulldozer

Politically and socially unaccountable, financial markets and transnationals make fundamental decisions about what we eat, what drugs we use, how we entertain ourselves, what corrupt regimes are to be supported with our money or how we treat the earth and its population. The lifestyle of the entire world is the target of a commercial carpet-bombing that threatens to annihilate traditions that go back even thousands of years. Colonised by the values of a superficial corporative culture, human needs are homogenised and recreated in line with the new oligarchy's own commercial needs. The American way of life as portrayed in films and television, still provincial in many ways, has turned into a standardised, commodified and dehumanised model to be copied. Its values and standards impose their imprint on a planetary scale, levelling off the world's separate fountains of imaginativeness.

The presence of the corporations is felt everywhere. 'M' for McDonald's, the high street ideogram of American culinary tawdriness and the image of our time's accelerated grimace, can be seen under the Parthenon in Athens or in St Mark's Square in Venice, where the smell of hamburgers and chips blends uncomfortably with the nostalgic strains of the little orchestra in the historic café next door. Wal-Mart has, likewise, built a supermarket next to the ruins of the giant pyramids built by Maya between the fifth and the ninth centuries. Wal-Mart entered Mexico's retail market in 1991, and now owns nearly one thousand department stores, all established with intention, as the company said, to bring lower prices for basic goods to consumers. The same is the case with the other American cultural icon, the Starbucks coffee shops – three thousand of them in Europe alone – which Howard Schultz, their founder, has turned into an international retailing phenomenon. 'One thing we don't need', the Italians retorted, 'is to be told by the Americans how to make good coffee.' Yet they are.

The 'blanding of cities' by large chains is, indeed, eroding and undermining everywhere whatever cultural differences still exist. Even on the small Greek island of Skyros the locals drink coca cola, entertain themselves with American films on video, and frequent bars and pubs rather than the old style tavernas and cafés. Young girls look as if they have just emerged from Harvey Nichols. The invasion of the island by an alien and aggressive culture subliminally undermines, meanwhile, the nature of the locals' relation with their past and their values, with their environment and with each other. It disconnects them from the springs of their wisdom and reshuffles their identity. The 'needs' of peoples beyond the island's own shores become their needs, and western values, which assess progress on the strength of the general models of historical development, unmediated by time, sweep aside all notions of organic development.

Wealth, which Freud said, brings so little happiness as 'money was not a wish in childhood', takes precedence over life; and the local art, culture, nature, history, customs, objectified in 'the tumult and the babble that sweeps us helpless in its vulgar tide', as Goethe, sitting in the timeless zone, cried, turn from a lived experience into a commodity for sale to the tourists. Neither of them are any longer what they were.

Separated from their original meaning, differentiated, subjected to mediation, they are all, as Georg Simmel argued in earlier times, objectified. Converted into a standing-reserve, Martin Heidegger emphasised, too, they become a resource for human consumption. Society's photo-album, kept to remind us what old ethical principles, now wrinkled and bent by time, looked like when they were young, has been mislaid; and nobody looks for it, for nobody seems to need it as unfettered capitalism and unadorned greed rather than old-fashioned principles will, we are led to believe, enable the spirit of man to fly higher. Cynicism, nurtured by the capitalist ethos which guides us in the belief that anything can be bought, is the inevitable result, anything but temporary for, once exposed to the globalising imperative, nothing is going to remain the same.

The constant 'updating' of our thinking is ensured at blinding speed by TV images and the film industry, all controlled by a small number of super-powerful American corporations – General Electric, Walt Disney, AOL-Time Warner, Viacom (formerly Westinghouse Electric Co) or News Corporation. They own, not just major TV networks, including NBC, ABC, CNN or CBS, but Hollywood in its entirety, book publishing companies, music companies, retail stores, amusement parks, magazines, newspapers and the like. Their market is global, for they control, not only production, but also distribution. Even the relatively successful British film industry has no control over the latter because it is almost entirely in the hands of the Hollywood moguls. American films reach up to 90 per cent of audiences in some European countries, in Africa two out of three films shown are American, British TV is saturated with American sitcoms and movies. Murdoch's satellites, with their heavy traffic of US audovisual content, saturate the Asian subcontinent. The Internet makes little difference. Thirteen of the fourteen top internet firms are American – number fourteen is British.

Disney's pasteurised images, the lowest possible common denominator which homogenises demand in order to win the middle ground with standardised services and products, uproot what millennia of tradition have created. In a world girdled by mass communications networks, the same goes for global information and entertainment, fashion and global lifestyles. Although people do not exactly lose their capacity for critical reflection, the global media's power cannot be counterbalanced. Transnational high-tech capitalism, the threat to diversity, pluralism, autonomy and the individual's right to be different, has broken through the gates of history as we knew it. Its unpromising inclination, free from scrupulous concerns, spiritually disabled, is the trial which individuals face while standing on their own, frail, debilitated, unequivocally impotent.

The impact of what is nothing less than brainwashing – one day to be achieved, if author Geoff Ryman is right, via an über-internet that beams messages directly into the brain – is devastating. It transforms societies mentally, culturally, socially, and even politically by promoting America's outlook, her biases, fears and prejudices, and also her priorities on the rest of the world. Political cultures are being transformed by the personality-driven American model, advertising and the lavish electoral spending of money or the shallowness of American democracy. The influence is often more direct than the time that, for example, the US launched an Arab-language television channel, Al Hurra, as a counterweight to Arab-run satellite stations that had proved highly popular to Washington's irk. Despite Arab opposition, Britain, too, expecting political dividends like the US, intends to run its own Arab-language TV channel 24 hours a day.

Heralded as an unprecedented opportunity for genuine and diverse cultural exchange, the means that will take us beyond the atomising rationality of the Gutenberg galaxy to the global village, a term coined in the 60's by Marshall McLuhan, planetary communication, the man himself said, acts as a cultural bulldozer. Planetary communication is a one-way dissemination of news and views – the satellite TV networks talk to the world, and we, speechless, have no option but to absorb the message. For the postmodernists, this is the end of man, of history, of the social, and of a culture in which people are able to relate to public events or see a connection between their own affairs and the destiny of mankind. As sharp as a kidney pain, this does not even need to be proven.

Profit, Peter Drucker, the management guru, wrote in his influential book *The Practice of Management*, 'is not the explanation, cause or rationale of business behaviour and business decisions, but the test of their validity.' Heedless of the wisdom embodied in this short sentence, hungry for profit, intoxicated like the conquistadors by their power to quell and root out, and oblivious to the concerns of all those outside their boardrooms, the multinationals erase difference throughout the world. As Marx predicted, through the exploitation of the world market, capitalism 'has given a cosmopolitan character to production and consumption in every country'– it has created 'a world after its own image'.

The optimists, foreseeing a global order, anarchic and spontaneous, free and good for those who can take advantage of it, are, of course, not missing. The promise of a better world is given by the globalisation's implicit promise to remove poverty, and by the newly-won, and yet for the libertarians still limited, freedom of individuals to be who they want to be, uninhibited by ideology, religion, convention, ethics or responsibility – the only connection is brand loyalty. The Other, an endangered species, is as important as the lost island of Atlantis. But the promise of a better world that goes hand-in-hand with the declaration of war upon all other cultures, even if it is to be met, cannot sweep aside human sensibilities, emotions that make people human and connections that give meaning to their lives. This is what the rich and powerful of this world fail abysmally to understand, and hence, when anger bursts forth, they greet it with incomprehension.

For a person like me, someone, in other words, who comes from a small country with a language which survived through the millennia, with a distinct culture of its own and with a prejudiced pride in its past, the preservation of difference is as important as life itself. My Greekness, the unbound reminiscences of a past, lived and still alive, the active cultural and spiritual memory linking me to traditions which are not even observed but, like Greece's poetry, are in my blood and also to emotions, this seething juice of life which puts colour on the cheeks of inexactitude, they all give me roots, a home and a sense of belonging; brand loyalty. They define me as much as the times we 'clenched our sorrows between rows of teeth that formed so many smiles' define my past, or as much as the banks define a river. They are me.

Being a historically situated entity, I am linked to the space where my ancestors are buried, to the pastel of Attica's landscape, to the scents of the mellow summer nights and the mellifluous breathing of the Aegean Sea in whose 'lustral waters', Greek poet Takis

Papatsonis testified, 'Zeus himself once delighted'. I am inseparable from the immense power of Theodorakis' music, Ritsos' poetry or Fasianos' paintings, all of them deeply rooted in my country's long tradition that stretches back thousands of years. None of these can be obliterated by the global powers' universal maxims. And if we ever reach a point that, swamped by another culture, my birthplace turns into an item in the world's archaeological museum that 'me' will disappear.

Yet, undermined by the alarming fragility of memories and the winds of change, constant in a world which technologically, socially, economically, militarily or culturally is being reshaped at breathtaking pace, cultures and the traditions on which they are founded are being swept away.

Significantly, however, unlike universal truths, those denounced by postmodernism, their disappearance is irreversible. The six hundred languages lost in the last one hundred years can woefully testify to it. Incidentally, at the present rate of destruction, only six hundred of the six thousand languages left are expected to be spoken at the end of the century. Considering, however, that, as the Californian teacher told his Latin pupils in Isabel Allende's *The Infinite Plan*, English was all Christ needed to write the Bible, one could also argue that we have five hundred and ninety-nine languages too many.

Acknowledging tradition, the struggles of all the dead generations, owning what the cooperation of generations has produced in terms of beliefs, customs and ways of behaving, does not involve an unreflective acceptance of the past. The past is anything but an unmixed blessing. Though some mechanisms for change are in place, traditional societies tend to nurture hierarchies, enforce their own code of conduct and resist any change that unsettles some sort of eternal order threatened by the capitalist eternity. Demanding conformity, they restrict the individual's autonomy, and, instinctively conservative, they discourage innovation. Uncomfortably, as one might deduce from the attitude of the British working class, which, unlike the outward-looking middle class, still looks inwards, tradition also carries with it hostility to homosexuality, ethnic and religious minorities, women or Europe.

But tradition is, on the other hand, important in a small country like Greece, where, Yannis Ritsos rather bitterly observed, one can see 'signs in foreign letters and also Greek lemon trees'. It is one of the very few defences left against the corporative cultural bulldozers and the American ideology masquerading as the global truth of our times.

Opting for what surrealist poet Nicos Engonopoulos called 'a revolution in the name of tradition', like-minded European countries such as France and Spain, thus, look for new ways to protect cultural diversity against US hegemony. They try to defend themselves, as Rilke said a long time ago, i.e. before people had everything but a life, against the latter's 'empty, indifferent things ... sham things, dummy life'. Having reached the conclusion that we have many pasts, but, it seems, only a single future dressed up in American colours, the chairman of the European parliament's culture committee stressed that 'the survival of the cultural identity of Europe is at stake'.

More dramatically, the leader of the Hungarian Democratic Forum party said not long ago that Budapest is being 'encircled by western culture and shopping malls as the city had once been rigged by Soviet tanks.' Even the Germans, who have traditionally resisted aspects of US pop culture, are worried at the activities of the multinationals, the 'locusts', as some called them. 'We should hold on to our culture', the prime minister of North Rhine Westphalia said when Vodafone bid for Mannesmann, 'and that applies to our business culture as well'; or the Japanese, who have called for English buzzwords to be banned from the country's language.

Sharing the same fears, people in several other countries resist the Americanisation of their culture and the dominance of big global corporations. 'If we're not careful', Dick Smith, the Australian millionaire entrepreneur, said, 'we will completely lose control of our destiny'. His 'Genuine Australian Foods' have taken the market by storm – a great many Australians are, it seems, almost as hostile to the American-led globalisation as the millions who have taken to the streets all over the world. Resentment of US foreign policy because of the Iraq war seems to have transferred to all things American and to be further eroding the global appeal of US brands and their global civilisation.

Making cultural diversity part of humanity's common heritage, Unesco stepped in with the Convention for the protection of the diversity of cultural contents and artistic expressions. Cultural goods and services, it declared, are 'vehicles of identity, values and meaning'. The Convention, which removes culture from the World Trade Organisation concerns, intends to protect movies, music and other cultural treasures from foreign competition. Denouncing it as unfairly obstructing the flow of ideas, goods and services across borders, the US voted against it. The Convention was nevertheless endorsed by 148 to 2 votes.

Globalisation can be accepted but only if all nations of the world feel part of the big family, equally respected and honoured in celebration of their common humanity. As former UN Secretary General Kofi Annan put it, the World Cup gives us the model. Anything other than this will only foster resentment, hostility, even rioting as some have already forecast.

But, meanwhile, and as the Iraq war has bolstered nationalism, other forms of opposition to globalisation have emerged. Muslims all over the world have strengthened their religious identity and non-Muslims have been creating new and often more rigid entities. Religious groupings have expressed themselves either violently as in the case of the Islamists, or by the erection of visible and invisible barriers to globalisation as in the case of Christian and Jewish fundamentalists.

Globalisation may be 'inevitable and irreversible', but its shape is anything but certain. The backlash to the unfettered and unrestrained markets' frontal assault on what matters to people most together with the new emphasis on localism make predictions difficult.

Back in 1851, Wilhelm Mommsen, the German historian, wrote: 'it is humanity's duty today to see that civilisation does not destroy culture', the latter being, as Max Weber, the German sociologist and philosopher, said, a set of normative principles, values and ideals as opposed to civilisation, a mass of practical, technical knowledge. One can say the same more forcefully today. For the new and subtle universalism of the multinationals is destroying culture. Antagonistic to both the community and the individual, it also disempowers them both, for the more global daily life gets, the less important they, and the more parochial their concerns, become. The individual, unable to relate personally to anything, much less to influence anything of substance, acknowledged by the system only as consumer, disconnected and marginalised, has no option but to withdraw into his private world with a good book, like this one, to read for inspiration.

Except that, as the young Greek novelist Panos Karnezis pointed out, people do not learn from books. Were they to, 'libraries would be closed to the public'.

5. The Voiceless Majority

Politics, Aristotle explained a long time ago, constitutes an unique public sphere in which people come together, interact, make decisions, forge citizen bonds, carry out the imperatives of change, and ultimately search for a better future. It was what I thought I was doing during those days before the Iraq war, when, together with millions, I opposed the fraud perpetrated in the name of what was euphemistically called 'war on terror', the illegitimate use of force, the dangerous doctrine of pre-emptive strikes and the planned slaughter of the untameable. The bullish vision of a US-controlled new world order and the pressure on the UN to abolish itself by rubber stamping decisions already taken by president Bush and prime minister Blair, with the support of, among others, US senator Hillary Clinton – Tony Blair in skirts – was as frightful as it was repugnant. I felt we had to stand up and tell the government 'No War', and that was what we did.

This 'us' included people from all walks of life, everybody who had a voice including schoolchildren, absent from the streets for a generation but now angry enough to rebel against authority and its false pretensions. The old-fashioned kind of march-and-rally, which had looked as outdated as the songs of Vera Lynn, the British forces' sweetheart during the Second World War, was back in vogue again. A new militancy was sweeping the country. More than four thousand people in Britain, a Sunday newspaper columnist wrote, had signed a pledge to support civil disobedience, such as blocking roads, when the war was expected to begin; the politicians, she wrote, are out of step with the people; the government faces a crisis of legitimacy.

Empowered by moral outrage, the force of their convictions, and the sheer size of a protest movement that had dwarfed anything that had ever taken place before, assertive and determined to claim back leadership and direction from an establishment that no longer represented them, people stormed the Bastille of politics. Generation Apathy had woken up, for as José Luis Rodríguez Zapatero, the Spanish prime minister, put it a year later, 'you cannot organise a war with lies.' Pessimism dissipated almost overnight. People did not just demand, but actually expected to be listened to. After all, nine out of ten according to a BBC poll conducted at the time, did not want the war pursued by the 'democratic imperialists', at least not without a second UN resolution. For a moment, it looked as if the age's impotence was just a nightmare from which everyone seemed to have emerged fresh, like spring water straight from the source, and ready to prove that decisions are within, and not beyond, the reach of citizens. The Americans, who like Rose in Margaret Atwood's *The Robber Bride*, would rather have others dig the mass graves, for they might break a nail, would have to fight 'evil' on their own.

But it was not to be. 'Democracy' triumphed and the 'evil dictator' was easily defeated. But so was civil society and our own political system. Arrogance, aggressiveness, bad faith, lesser calculations, spin, corruption, incompetence, ambitions, hidden interests, bullying, bribing, cajoling and blackmailing, going hand-in-hand with a cynical contempt for public opinion and utter disregard for the most fundamental features of our democratic institutions sent the pervasive disillusionment with the system to new depths. Prime minister Blair had successfully attacked not so much Saddam Hussein as the people he was elected to represent, their commitment to some higher principle, the giving and most generous part of themselves. Thus he increased even further the ethical, moral and political deficit of the country's system. Even the resulting institutional crisis, or what I saw as an institutional crisis, a crisis of authority, was not as bad as his betrayal of the country's expectations.

Some did, of course, claim that his decision to take the country to war demanded courage. But 'courage', as Euripides said, 'is not looking friends in the face after betraying them. This is not even audacity; it's a disease.'

Decisions turned out once again to be beyond the reach of the people. They are the exclusive privilege of institutionalised power, rigid and unresponsive to the sentiments of those it is supposed to represent, but also spineless, self-seeking and corrupt. Contemporary politics has left no room for the effective participation of the people in the exercise of power. Having given way to 'McPolitics', politics is now a dumbed-down, one-dimensional relationship between the prime minister, a new class of professional politicians unwilling to challenge the leader whose patronage is the key to higher office, and an insatiable media, with the rest of us reduced to spectators, bit players and cheerleaders.

'Power', Lord Wilson, former secretary of the Cabinet and head of UK's civil service under Labour, said, is now gripped 'much more tightly within relatively few hands' – New Labour 'staged a coup, first of all against the Labour party, and then against the processes of government.' Parliament, this 'toothless granny', is there only to rubber stamp decisions taken, not by the government, but by our own 'beloved leader'. Even the Cabinet, Lord Butler, cabinet secretary when Labour swept into power in 1997, took no more than one decision in the first eight months in office, and this was to leave the decision on the Millennium Dome to the prime minister. Such a system, Cornelius Castoriades held, can no longer be called 'democracy'. It is 'a liberal oligarchy'. Politicians, Demosthenes, the fourth century BC Athenian statesman, said before him, imagine that they sell everything but themselves only to discover that they have sold themselves first.

The erosion of the people's power to influence events following the closure of the public sphere goes hand in hand with the concentration of power in the hands of increasingly fewer individuals, those controlling the bureaucracy, the media and above all corporate capitalism. Multinational corporations dominate the decision-making process – the market, even if well regulated, will always control the crucial areas of investment flow and resource allocation. This process, brilliantly documented by Noreen Hertz in *The Silent Takeover*, has turned national politicians into guilty bystanders, unable to check the multinationals' activity and, thereby, the economy of their own countries. 'Governments can be held to account', a leader in the *Financial Times* pointed out rather bluntly, 'but they no longer seem to run the show.'

In some instances, even the semblance has gone – guns, tobacco, sweatshops and even high technology industries are totally beyond the reach of regulatory bodies. This crony capitalism and its moneyed interests can, meanwhile, afford the best politicians money can buy through contributions to presidential campaigns, 'loans' or backhanders offered by huge companies to politicians in so many countries.

Politics, which in my early days I thought of as something like a Freudian death wish in support of an erotic attachment to life, has been reduced to a branch of business. It has ended up as a mechanism for choosing managers capable of solidifying the 'flexible market' and protecting its interests both at home and abroad. 'Crudely put', Boris Berezovsky brutally said, 'capital hires the authorities for work. The form of hiring is called elections.' Berezovsky is the Russian tycoon whom many Russians view as the incarnation of 'robber capitalism'. His description of the electoral process may have the kind of bad breath, which, like Tartuffe's looks, can stop the church clock. Yet he was only making a speech in favour of a notion that had already been passed.

The threat the big money guns pose to the system, and also society, is naturally very civilised. There are no brownshirts roaring drunk in the streets, for people do things together but they are not together to represent a threat, and no media censorship, for nobody listens to anything or anybody any more. Public debates, media soundbites which distort, even obliterate, public concerns, are something like public conveniences for thought relief – 'pure hubbub', Primo Levi would have said, 'to pretend that silence is not silence'. Moreover, nobody is, or will be, asked to show his passport before crossing a street, or declare his love of daffodils to the police. The dominant class no longer needs to force the dominated to conform to its will. Its power, embodied in all social practices and institutions, in habits too loyal to us, or, as Antonio Gramsci said, in the lived order of culture, is just reproduced by it. 'Custom', Pindar had already clarified, 'is king over all.'

Without a grand design or a guiding vision, which the 'war on terror' fails to provide, rather than a means to an end politics has become an end in itself; and politicians, rather than win elections to implement policies, formulate policies to win elections. This market-led approach, which treats the citizens as consumers, is the Gospel of the day, endorsed even by academics such as Vernon Bogdanov, professor of government at Oxford University – 'a party of the left', he wrote, 'can only hope to prosper if it bases its policies on a real understanding of popular aspirations', the latter being fashioned, of course, by the market-led consumerism. This is exactly what Tony Blair did by nurturing the individualistic, acquisitive culture of his time and the patriotism-cum-social-conservatism that brought Margaret Thatcher to power in 1979.

Elections, where all is decided, are often entertainment, showbiz promoted by agents and advertising companies, media events designed to expand our comfort zone. Professional entertainers have, indeed, in some instances been replacing faceless politicians in the parties' efforts to generate some interest in the moribund political system. Actors Arnold Schwarzenegger, in California, Fernando Poe Jr, in the Philippines, or even Italian prime minister Silvio Berlusconi, a former cruise ship entertainer, offer striking examples of populist campaigns against a discredited political establishment. In Japan, I read, among those running for election were a former professional wrestler called Tiger Mask, singers, novelists, a failed dotcom entrepreneur and a television personality.

With democracy missing the bodily substance to gratify the spirit of its citizens, politics, as a result, is no longer about competing political philosophies. It is, instead, about competing political nuances represented by competing political élites, all children of the middle class for whom politics is a career. Its definition is no longer given in terms of political, ethical or moral values. It is, instead, drawn in terms of institutional rules which ostensibly create limits to power, and procedures which theoretically ensure the smooth functioning of its institutions. Even so the failure is overwhelming because the face of corruption is often the face of our political culture as, for example, was the case in the US with lobbyist Jack Abramoff, who bribed politicians with millions of dollars to buy influence over policy. Abramoff was for politics what Enron was for business.

Just a generation ago, three out of four people trusted the government would 'do the right thing most of the time'. In 2000 their number fell to two out of ten, and in the post-Iraq era it sank even further. It could hardly be otherwise when elected leaders are caught lying without shame as president Nixon did with his 'I am not a crook', president Clinton with his 'I did not have sexual relations with that woman' or president George W. Bush with his 'Saddam's weapons of mass destruction'. Contempt for politics and politicians could not become much more pronounced.

Hence elections do not mean a thing. Conducted in a professionals' bubble, floating in a sea of voters' indifference, they are only the embodiment of the existing democratic deficit, for people appoint and governments disappoint. If elections could change anything, London mayor Livingstone has said, they would have been banned. Myself, I cannot even use my right to vote, won in costly battles by previous generations, for there is nobody among the figures of the political establishment I can identify with. None of them represents me as this 'me' manifests itself in this book, a book which, incidentally, 'will not pay for the cigars I smoked writing it', as Marx prophesied about his own book, *Capital*. Without a cigar in his mouth, Marx, incidentally, looked, as novelist John Fowles would say, like a yacht without a mast.

Unable to identify with the social and political entity, alienated from it, even hostile to its fate, citizens thus opt out massively from the political process. They do not even want to know about it – American professor Bryan Caplan called this phenomenon 'rational ignorance'. Despite free haircuts or cinema tickets offered as inducements by Russian president Putin many refused even to vote. The 76% of the electorate who bothered to vote in 1979, when Margaret Thatcher won power to revive the animal spirits of the middle class, was reduced to 71.5% in 1997, the year Tony Blair came to power to help the rich become richer, declined further still to 58% in the 2001 elections. At 61%, the turnout in 2005 was slightly improved but was still the third lowest since 1847. The record is worse in the US where only one in two people turn out to vote – in the 2000 presidential elections the turnout was 51.3%. The gap between politicians and people, particularly those representing the newer generation, has never been as great – and that is not just in the UK and the USA, but all over the world, from Russia to Malawi.

What was described once as the 'silent' majority has turned into the voiceless majority. Hence the diminution of the importance of being a citizen actively involved in the affairs of the state, and the apathy and the disenchantment of large sections of the European public with mainstream politics. Hence also the swing in favour of extreme right wing populists, so disturbingly evident in France, Austria, Holland, Italy or Denmark, and the possible emergence of a populist, power-hungry CEO politician, a super-manager, who will use mass communication techniques to entertain and mass-surveillance systems to overpower dissent. We have, as Carl Boggs, the American political theorist, stated, reached 'the end of politics'.

Submerged into the vacuous cosmopolitanism of our time, the citizens, depoliticised, find themselves unable to commit to a common project. To do so, they need to feel that their society is theirs, which they do not, and to be able to identify with something called 'home', which they cannot. The only unifying force is the market – 'with money in the pocket', Moll Flanders, the character in a Daniel Defoe novel, said, 'one is at home anywhere.' The result is the fragmentation of the whole, and disintegration, not just of social structures, but, as Charles Taylor pointed out, of contemporary democracies as well. The problem has, however, disappeared in the unnamed streets of money.

Present in the political process as a largely passive observer of a closed system, the public both is seen and sees itself as a market. The voters-consumers, economist Fred Hirsch said, seek the store that offers the best prices – 'we're selling a product like anyone else', a Minister in Tony Blair's government said soon after the 1997 elections, 'and it's critical to get across the right corporate image.' With the democratic process reduced to mere commerce, the citizens are no longer citizens, but consumers, manipulated by vested interests and lobbies, told what is important, flattered, placated and brainwashed, and, naturally, encouraged to talk about sex, the flag and the foetus, who does what to whom, when and how.

Politics has been degraded to talk about personalities, scandals, sleaze, intrigue, gossip and spin. What matters is 'style', image, the perception of everything in terms of hollow abstractions worked out by public relations consultants and spin doctors. A day before the UK national elections of 2001, the New Labour spin machine produced a photograph of Cherie Blair, the prime minister's wife, catnapping for the camera on her husband's shoulder aboard his helicopter, while the man, fully alert, was involved with his paperwork. The sense of family harmony and also purpose, utterly overwhelming, must certainly have been worth a few dozen extra votes.

Precluded from effective participation in the affairs of the state, the citizens have become the power to be won if the system is to maintain its legitimacy. 'You, my people', novelist Margaret Atwood in vain bewails, 'defrauded me of hope and left me alone with politics', the unsurvivable condition. Erasmus was said to get nauseous at the smell of fish. I feel likewise at the smell of party politics.

The citizen-consumers can, of course, roar in protest like flies or write a letter to *The Guardian*, on which they can always expand during an after-dinner chat. But the agenda of any public discussion is set by the status quo – and never threatens it. Democracy, though generally acclaimed as the only system which empowers the people, is still the best, except that in its current dysfunctional form it does instead more to disempower them. In our day, this is the case almost by definition as modern politics has, indeed, become increasingly irrelevant to the everyday life of the individual. For whatever the government says, we still have to lead a life alienated from our work, cities, inner self or spirit, we still have to win our self-respect in terms dictated by the consumer culture, and we still have to sit in traffic jams breathing the carbon-monoxide filled air with which we cool our porridge the next day.

Scientised, de-politicized, de-ideologized and managerialised in a way which is both more pervasive and more difficult to detect, democracy, agoraphobic, has taken politics out of politics. The management of what is left is in the hands of the shadowy techno-bureaucratic élite, the quangos and an unelected coterie of advisers who know best the 'right' social and political choices, which they love to present as 'technical'. Far from being cushioned by the system, democracy is, indeed, threatened by it, by the emerging technofascism. Postmodernist Peter Mandelson, the *eminence grise* of New Labour, in a sense underlined this when, in 1998, he prophesied that the 'era of pure representative democracy may be coming to an end'.

Looking through the postmodernist telescope far into the future, beyond the Second Coming and Going, all we have been told to expect is ferocious, merciless political battles on the best way to boil an egg. The new world and its global order, Michael Hardt and Toni Negri argued in their book *Empire*, has effectively suspended history and thereby fixed the existing state of affairs to eternity. 'The democratic class struggle', American professor Seymour Martin Lipset, had said earlier, 'will continue, but it will be a fight without ideologies'. Daniel Bell, another American, author of *The End of Ideology*, diagnosed the 'exhaustion of political ideas', and Richard Rorty, the US Stanford University 'neopragmatic' postmodernist, claimed that liberal democracy does not need any philosophical justification. The age of ideology is dead, as dead, perhaps, as the pencil, whose demise was confidently predicted by the *New York Times* in 1938. To the dismay of all those good women without history, history is null and void.

Francis Fukuyama, the best known proponent of 'the end of ideology' thesis until Tony Blair's arrival, argued, likewise, that the advanced countries 'have no alternative model of political and economic organisation other than democratic capitalism.' The assumption, made in 1989 at the end of the cold war, and at that stage as safe as extolling the virtues of the dead, rested, however, on a contradiction: capitalism, seen by many as a condition of democracy, striving for profit, has little, if anything, to do with Justice which is the essence of democracy.

The postmodernist era made no room for new movements, new structures or dreams. In its barren, vacuous ground nothing grows. The clock has stopped – time is taking a rest. Presumably, we are not going through another phase in the history of mankind, but through a final phase which will end all phases. *Conclamatum est.* The Messiah may still come, but God will get rid of him. However, speculation about the end of ideology, often called philosophy, cannot tell the end of a story which has not even been conceived. History, the history of our misfortunes and miscalculations, is hardly likely to die of boredom. 'Cities and thrones and powers', Rudyard Kipling, the English novelist and poet, pondered, 'stand in time's eye almost as long as flowers which daily die.'

The future will most certainly not see the end of the struggle between Good and Evil even if Rupert Murdoch, the Australian-born world media mogul, makes us pay to see it. After all, nobody, not even those in the prophecy business, can read the future.

All one can predict with certainty is rain at Wimbledon.

6. In Nemesis Avenue

Addicted to profit like an alcoholic to alcohol, the free market would stop at nothing to serve its addiction. Hence the disregard of the plight of the vulnerable, and the terrible injustices done to the 'Other', whether the 'Other' is the planet, people, the world's cultures or the principle of equality among nations. Hence also its blindness to the world's gross inequalities and the new top-bottom divides or its inherent inability to understand that economic growth is neither desirable nor sustainable. US policy, in particular, simple as a Madeira cake, has only managed to polarise the conflict by attacking those who do not have anything, not even a birthday. Justice and equality, which Naomi Klein, the Canadian author, said are 'the most sustainable strategies against violence and fundamentalism', are arrogantly and foolishly dismissed. Excess is glorified. Greed, in partnership with fear, make the law of the land.

The chorus in Aeschylus' *Agamemnon* warned us: 'impious acts breed their own kind; and evil's nature is to multiply.' Yet the US seems impervious to it, or, to the extent she seems to take notice, she responds only militarily. However, even if sustained by overwhelming power, injustice committed when the physical or moral equilibrium is disturbed, is bound to provoke violent reactions. Hybris invites only retribution – Nemesis, the remorseless Goddess, who in Greek mythology is the personification of the moral reverence for law, is never too far away. Crimes cannot be committed with impunity, and inordinate good fortune cannot be enjoyed for ever without expiation. The process is always painful, but the balance between all the elements of the equilibrium has to be restored if things are not to fall apart. The Earth itself, grossly abused by humans, takes the lead in this respect.

As the Intergovernmental Panel on Climate Change emphasised 'unequivocally' in the spring of 2007, man-made global warming will set in motion irreversible and frightening natural processes unless carbon dioxide emissions are curbed by 2020. The significant increase in temperatures, which occurred despite the industrialised world's commitments made at the Rio de Janeiro Earth Summit in 1992, and the Kyoto Protocol of 1997, is bound to cause the melting of the ice shields in Greenland, rising sea-levels and the over-acidification of the oceans. Should that not be enough, we may, likewise, expect floods, fierce hurricanes, heatwaves and long and intense droughts, fires and pest outbreaks, all of which will reduce foodstocks worldwide, lead to the extinction of many animal species and fuel a number of diseases such as malaria and yellow fever. The human crisis these developments will cause will be measured by massive increases in poverty and hunger beyond anything the world has ever seen.

The panel did not mention the political fallout of such developments, but it does not take a prophet to see widespread rioting, even civil wars and wars between states for the most essential things, food and water, that make the difference between life and death. The likelihood that these conflicts will turn into a much bitter struggle between the First and the Third world over resources, and also refugees trying to escape their deadened lands to the north, has already raised its ugly head.

Temperatures could rise further if 'feedback' effects take place, such as the thawing of Siberian permafrost leading to the release of large quantities of methane, a greenhouse gas more potent than carbon dioxide. Worst hit are expected to be the poor countries – Bangladesh, Vietnam, India and China who is expected to be the biggest emitter of greenhouse gases in 2009, i.e. hardly those who have caused the problem in the first place as most of greenhouse gases emitted since the industrial revolution have come from Europe and the US. Ironically, northern Europe is expected to be the winner from the rising temperatures but not without damage to its vital infrastructure – road and rail networks, water and energy systems and healthcare. On the other hand, England may well grow bananas for export to Equador and Scotland make wine for the Spaniards.

Carbon dioxide emissions are already the prime cause of, among other things, climate-related disasters which, according to the World Health Organisation, cause in turn 150,000 untimely deaths a year – thousands perished in France alone during the 2003 heatwave – and a worldwide epidemic of asthma. Traffic fumes, The Lancet, the UK medical journal, reported, account for one in twenty deaths in Europe. Smog further causes damage to health, crops and wildlife.

The Kyoto Protocol, to which the US still objects, can hardly slow global warming as the more carbon dioxide, the main greenhouse gas, penetrates the atmospheric concentrations, the more the ozone layer which protects the earth from cancer-causing ultraviolet radiation is being depleted. Emissions trading, vulnerable to gaming by big business and governments alike, even providing free emission allowances and windfall profits for some, has meanwhile manifestly failed to arrest global warming.

Nevertheless, many newly industrialised nations, the members of the Organisation of Petroleum Exporting Countries, and the USA, Canada, Australia and Japan, are still reluctant to endorse strict commitments on cutting emissions and stop the global warming, a crime against the planet. Consumer societies, Austrian economist Joseph Schumpeter wrote, are abandoning the future to indulge in the present.

The US in particular, by far the biggest polluter, refusing to stand 'shoulder to shoulder' with the rest of the world, disavowed unanimously the Kyoto Protocol and consistently obstructed any progress towards an agreement to reduce carbon dioxide emissions. Any such proposals, she made clear even as late as May 2007, are 'fundamentally incompatible' with the US president's views. The American refusal to join the fight against climate change was backed up with the argument that the Protocol was a European plot to undermine US competitiveness as it did not demand an emission reduction from China, India, Brazil and other developing nations, all those beyond the south wind.

The starting point of the negotiations which led to the conclusion of the Kyoto agreement had been lost. 'We've forgotten the beginning of your speech and couldn't understand the end', the Spartans, unwilling to help the Samians against Polycrates, their tyrant, answered the Samian delegation in similar fashion.

The US, whose 5 per cent of the world's population accounts for 25 per cent of carbon emissions, has been unwilling to meet her obligations. The developing countries, reluctant to be locked in a position of inferiority merely because others exploited global absorptive capacity first, are equally unwilling to give way or, at least, to set mandatory targets. As unwilling to fall into line are also several new EU members from eastern Europe. Of course, under intense pressure both at home and abroad, US president Bush, prompted, as he said, by new scientific findings, declared an interest in the subject. His late Damascene conversion, which was met only with incredulity, ensured nevertheless a commitment on his part at the G8 summit in Heiligendamm, the luxury resort on Germany's Baltic Sea coast, to join the United Nations conference in Bali later in 2007 in search of a successor to the Kyoto protocol.

As one might expect, the Bali conference failed to produce any reference to targets on emission reductions or decide how the burden of cutting emissions should be shared between the developed and the developing world. No commitments involving quantifiable pledges on temperatures and greenhouse emissions could be made. But at least all 187 countries, including the US, China and India, agreed that a comprehensive agreement had to be negotiated by 2009 to prevent the forthcoming and also dangerous climate change. However, if the Bali conference itself is anything to go by, one can only expect too little too late.

President Bush, just like nearly everybody else, is committed to 'progress'. In the name of this progress, however, the environment, once thought of as the mother of all life, is systematically being ravaged; the planet's resources, created over millions of years, are being ruthlessly plundered; and future generations, faced with this structural bias against them, are deprived of what they need in order to survive. Mankind, WWF, the conservation group, said, is consuming twenty per cent more natural resources than the earth can produce. 'We are spending nature's capital faster than it can regenerate it.' Overexploitation of natural resources increases the likelihood of sudden changes such as regional climate shifts, the emergence of new diseases, drops in water quality, 'dead' zones in seas or the collapse of fisheries. 'One more the Prussians won't have', said the farmer who was determined to finish his stock of wine before the collapse of France. We seem to deal with the future as if it were the Prussians.

The process, antagonistic to the natural conditions of human existence, vicious and endless, has already created a crisis. Even at zero growth, this is a life without a future. Miserably, man, as Anton Chekhov, the Russian dramatist, observed as far back as 1879, has not been a creator – only a destroyer. 'Forests', he wrote, 'keep disappearing, rivers dry up, wildlife's becoming extinct, the climate's ruined and the land grows poorer and uglier every day.' The biodiversity, on which we all depend, is alarmingly decreasing together with the native cultures which sustain it as the developing nations, i.e. all those who have booked the cheaper seats in the world's theatre, receive no assistance whatsoever in order to stop killing wild animals for food or razing forests to the ground to cultivate biofuels. They are not helped by Western loans or guarantees either, as their main beneficiaries end up being the multinationals in construction, armaments, infrastructure equipment or air transport – all willing to help with anything inappropriate to the development of the Third World as long as it pays.

The world, a study in the journal *Science* warned in 2004, is experiencing the sixth mass extinction in its history. The activities of *homo sapiens*, Leakey and Lewin point out in *The Sixth Extinction*, their highly readable book, are so dangerous that half the present species on earth will become extinct by the end of this century. Considering that species cannot survive on their own, it is, thus, just possible that man has made his own survival impossible. In such a case we are already 'the living dead'. Apparently, in dealing with nature, our world, 'hooded hordes swarming over endless plains, stumbling in cracked earth', is one of perverts. Physical limits are not respected. Nothing is being spared. Hence the truly frightening response of 'Mother Earth'.

The injustice done to the earth that forces nature to be our nemesis is matched by the injustices done to humans as profits come before any moral standards. Nemesis, the force ready 'to avert', according to the Orphic lyrics, 'the dire, unfriendly race of counsels impious, arrogant and base', may again be just around the corner. 'Individuals', Philostratus, one of the leading sophists of the Roman world, tells us, 'cannot exalt themselves above humanity.'

Yet cynically, corrupt activities which enrich a few individuals at the expense of everybody else make headlines all the time. Scandals involving cooking the books to keep the share price up erupt continuously as do scandals involving insider trading – about one in four of takeover announcements in 2005 were preceded by suspicious share price movements that indicated possible insider trading. Ethics and governance are reduced to a box ticking exercise, useless for any purposes other than giving the corporations some good free publicity.

Lack of accountability and transparency has led to a succession of breathtaking corporate scandals: Andersen, Enron, WorldCom, Qwest Communication, Ahold, Parmalat, Nortel Networks – one unsavoury disaster after another in what can only be described as a corporate crime epidemic. On their way to grace, ten of Wall Street's biggest investment banks, including Citigroup's Salomon Smith Barney Unit, Credit Suisse First Boston and Merrill Lynch, were found guilty of fraud, and in many other instances companies broke trading rules to enable big investors to profit at the expense of small investors. Corporations such as British Airways, Virgin Atlantic, Lufthansa and other airlines colluded to set fuel surcharges on cargo and passenger flights at the expense of the consumer on whose behalf ostensibly the free market operates.

Banks and multinationals have, meanwhile, successfully exploited tax avoidance schemes to minimise their corporation tax liabilities with some of them paying nothing. And, in spite of the proliferation of corporate governance codes and a flourishing ethics business, schemes of bribery and corruption fit for the 21st century keep coming up: BAE Systems, Siemens, Total, Citigroup, AIG, Volkswagen, DaimlerChrysler or SK Corp – they all had to defend themselves against allegations of unethical misconduct. Lahmeyer, the German engineering consultancy group was actually found by the European Bank of Reconstruction and Development guilty of bribery in Lesotho and blacklisted as was Vetco International, the British oil and gas services company, found guilty in the US of bribery in Nigeria and fined $26m.

It looks as if the world can no longer tolerate standards. Even those willing to commit themselves to standards cannot do so without incurring pretty high costs. The European Investment Bank, its president said, had as a result of its policies lost business to Chinese banks because they apply lower ethical and environmental standards. Despite its declarations, on the other hand, the government of Tony Blair had no difficulty cancelling the investigation into the grossly unethical practices which allegedly featured in the British Aerospace Industry's dealings with Saudi Arabia. The message, fifty UK-based non-governmental organisations said, is that companies can 'bribe with impunity'.

In spite of all the talk about ethics, corporate culture rather than punish seems to reward unethical behaviour – honesty, integrity, transparency and public trust remain as elusive as Saddam's weapons of mass destruction. Rather than being brought under control, fraud and corruption are, indeed, worsening in both industrialised and developing countries, with rich élites using corruption structures to maintain gross inequalities between rich and poor, and public officials abusing their power to corrupt ends. Anything illegal is, of course, expected to be dealt with by the criminal justice system. But disgraceful behaviour which is not strictly-speaking illegal is nobody's business. Hence Jeffrey Skilling, former chief executive of the bankrupt energy trader Enron, was within his rights when he insisted that he would keep producing a product that might cause harm, or even death, to people who used it, because his job as a businessman was only 'to maximise return to the shareholders'. His words simply echo the wisdom of Milton Friedman, the principal exponent of monetarism, who insisted the main responsibility of managers is to maximise profits for the shareholders.

Immorality in the public domain, just like bad taste, cannot, of course, be arrested through legislation. The distinction between moral law and criminal law cannot be erased, and moral wrongs cannot be legally sanctioned as judicial wrongs unless we are willing to end up with a tyrannical state. Yet the crisis of modern capitalism is spiritual and moral rather than environmental, economic, political or social except that it is not recognised as such. Liberated from restraints, its current policies look as normal as sitting down for a rest.

Democracy in such a disequilibriated world is making way, meanwhile, to forces that it is unable to control. One of them, the globalised media barons, all of them with direct and extensive ties to big business, and all of them able to shape public opinion by giving people 'what they want', are intent in making us love our servitude to corporate profit. Never guilty of overestimating the taste of their readers or their viewers, the media will not fail to display a smelly patriotism or, often, cross the borders between fact and fiction. Newspapers, prime minister Tony Blair acknowledged but only in the last few days of his premiership, fight for a share of a shrinking market, and in doing so, they are 'increasingly and to a dangerous degree driven by impact'. Impact, incidentally, was the driving force behind his own government's culture of spin and his readiness to capitulate to the manufactured moral panic of the tabloids. 'Impact' has, of course, no respect for truth, except that lies, which arrive electronically as opposed to the truth which comes to us by foot, lie in the foundations of totalitarianism.

Driven by impact, the media cannot even be trusted to present the news without turning it into showbiz often involving emotional manipulation. Typical in this respect were the stories about the 2004 tsunami that hit the countries bordering on the Indian ocean which became the story of our astoundingly nice reaction to it, the story of the 'big-hearted Brits'. The media, in any case, do not reflect reality, as they claim; instead, being a force of their own, they shape it. And they do not give us 'what we want'. True, they are the mirror image of our society, but at the same time, rather than our responsibility, they cultivate our voyeurism and mould society in their own cynical, sensational and judgemental image. A cynical, mercenary, demagogic press will nevertheless produce inevitably in time a people as base as itself.

The threat posed to democracy by the corporations manifests itself in numerous ways. Even human cloning, whether for reproductive or therapeutic purposes but bound to lead in any case to the creation of supermen, is the prerogative of 'experts' and their employers, the corporations, all beyond any democratic control. So are the tumultuous and frightening advances in technology – particularly in nanotechnology and artificial intelligence – which, the majority of Americans believe, 'could take over the world'.

But rather than follow the moral instinct, sanitise our actions and re-balance our priorities we are focusing, instead, on the 'war on terror', which only aggravates the precarious situation we find ourselves in. Rather than Justice, the only foundation of a safe world, the objective is security, which can never be achieved without reference to Justice. The inevitable backlash has only made matters worse.

Defined even in its most narrow terms, this war, launched so improvidently and inadvisedly, does not work. The 'coalition of the willing' has disintegrated whether in Iraq or the Nato-led mission in Afghanistan, and the US is being forced into retreat. Meanwhile, the invasion of Iraq has unleashed the forces of Islamic extremism which redefined the struggle of the Muslims to assert themselves against all odds as a battle for their religion. Religion, the refuge of those who no longer find meaning in this world, is, in any case, undergoing a resurgence worldwide. In the United States more than four out of ten people describe themselves as born-again Christians, in Africa there is a proliferation of churches, especially Pentecostal and charismatic ones, in Latin America religion has openly, as in Paraguay, become a vibrant political force. According to a study by a Brazilian university, the number of evangelists in Brazil has risen from 4.8m in 1970 to an estimated 43.6m in 2007.

At a different time, the corruption of the democratic institutions would have led to the growth of a fascist movement. Although not mutually exclusive since human rights are often denied by religion, too, it is religion that is taking the lead right now.

The Iraq invasion and its aftermath has further highlighted the shortcomings of, but also undermined further, US policy. Preservation of the unipolar system by force if and when necessary, including preventive wars even in the absence of immediate threats, rather than strengthen, has weakened American influence worldwide. The world simply refuses to be bullied. Unconvinced that US political, military and economic power is a benevolent force, many countries seem moreover determined to reduce American influence – hence regional groups from Europe to Asia and South America are deepening their economic ties, and cut out American involvement in many projects. American isolation is even more pronounced in other areas, from trade and culture to human rights. Other countries, like Iran, try to raise to unacceptable levels the cost of another military venture, in Iran this time. Rather than heal the traumas produced by the divisions of the world, US policy helps only in the spiralling of things out of control.

Partly in response to the messy results their policy of conquest has produced, the Americans are now considering the deployment of their 'Star Wars' defensive shield in Poland and the Czech Republic. The UK is, likewise, thinking of replacing the Trident nuclear weapon systems with new, more advanced ones, that could, in turn, justify other States' own efforts to acquire nuclear weapons. In response to US unilateralism and the growing reliance of other powers on military force, Russia, on her part, warned that unless the US drops plans to site the system in eastern Europe, she might withdraw from the 1987 Intermediate-Range nuclear Forces treaty, which outlawed an entire class of medium-range weapons, and re-target Europe. China, likewise, has decided to modernise its armed forces. Almost cheerfully, the world is about to enter a new arms race to back the insanity of its actions.

Meanwhile, power on a global scale, which is being rapidly diffused, seems certain to lead to a new, multipolar world with China, India, Russia and Brazil among the new global players. Going through what former US secretary of state Madeleine Albright called 'a systemic change', the world looks increasingly uncertain, miles beyond the point the American display of raw military power had imagined it would be. To some, it looks already ungovernable.

Following the September 11 events and the new concerns that emerged, the anti-globalisation movement was forced to give way to a new movement determined to stop the idiotic 'war on terror'. Despite its unprecedented force, it did, however, fail to achieve its objectives, and at the end, even the monstrous nature of the escalated conflict could not bring the millions back onto the streets. Cynicism, even disgust at the political process, followed by resignation and apathy put the breaks to the search for a world fit for humans rather than as capitalism's raw material and the US's advanced weapon systems' unhappy beneficiaries. It seems as we have reached again a kind of dead end.

Yet the choice between a life lived in harmony with our environment and the hell of our separation from it, a personal world as a network of human relationships and a web of moneyed interests, and a humanity living in justice and peace and a world bent on self-destruction is more vital than ever. Except that nobody asks us to make it. The choices given are only those offered on 'interactive' television. The task under the circumstances, French sociologist Alain Touraine said, is to build what he called the 'movement', the mobilisation of convictions linked to the better part of ourselves, to force the pace against the forces of destruction.

Activating civil society again so that it can at least become a force able to control governments, corporations and institutions at least partially is, however, a tall order. If this unrivalled mobilisation of millions of people against the Iraq war failed to sway the UK government, what more can the citizens do to make their point heard? How can they be included in, rather than excluded from, the decision making process, and influence the course of the events? By voting George W. Bush out and Hillary Clinton in? By blogging their way through the Net? Or, failing all else, by turning into suicide bombers? The answer at this point is disheartening, but the moment is not eternity. Indeed, in our age of discontinuity every new day the face of the world is different from that of any other day.

Even if all our hopes and half of our fears come true, the future looks anything but promising. As Cassandra, the Trojan princess, said, 'there's no escape, none, once the hour's come.' But even if this is true, as true as the law of gravity, I would still not give up. Despite the five-star advice always available, one does not always have to be 'rational'. 'Rationality', the madness of modernism, feasting on its own flesh, threatens our existence. For better or worse, one's real needs as determined by one's inner self are not always compatible with survival and its tedious routines, jaundiced confrontations and odious compromises. To use the graceful verse of Randall Jarrell, the American poet and critic, 'even if the world should end tomorrow I still would plant my little apple-tree.'

Man always has a choice; actually, Jean-Paul Sartre said, he is condemned to be free.

Part III: The Challenge

1. Unlessened by Time

Motivating humans to assert themselves over their creations, God, systems, structures, wealth, technology or consumer goods, as well as over their own silent realities, can possibly one day give us, as poet Odysseus Elytis would have said, 'the soil back to our feet'. But this requires nothing less than the shifting of the tectonic plates of our culture, a peaceful cultural revolution that will reconnect our world to the sanity of the early days and the initial aspirations.

The challenge is not practical, as an issue-oriented campaign would probably argue. In a world self-obsessed and outer-directed, face to face with greed and aggression, vulgar commercialisation and rampant materialism, superficiality, irrationality, nihilism, destruction, meaninglessness, loneliness, alienation, depoliticisation, disempowerment and because of all this with religious fundamentalism, it is primarily spiritual and cultural. It is a challenge to our psyche. To meet it, we need to rediscover who and what we are – indeed, what is the essence of being human. This may well involve a journey to the roots of our existence, the primitive creative part of ourselves which dissolves and recomposes reality understood by earlier cultures but lost in the process of industrialisation and the indeterminacy of our times. It may also require for its successful conclusion a new innocence of perception, suntanned by the primordial awareness of earlier times and free from the restrictions of habitual and repressive conceptual frameworks. If the Freudians are right, this will happen when we have recovered what was lost when individuation split consciousness and the unconscious.

While waiting for the reunion of the latter two, which may be the day we will reown our barbarity, we might, however, look back in history – and, perhaps, if the Americans can be persuaded, a little further back than 1909, the year Henry Ford produced his famous Model T. As Marcuse held, 'no persuasion, no theory, no reasoning can break this prison (of subjectivity), unless the fixed, petrified sensibility of the individuals is "dissolved", opened to a new dimension in history.' The past, E.P. Thompson argued, too, 'can sustain the present and prefigure possibilities'. It can remind us of our unfulfilled dreams and forgotten aspirations. It may also teach us how to make the same old mistakes again, but this time better.

But the past has no firm beginnings – it is hard to tell when history begins. One may well start with the Shamanic world of spirits, a world whose beliefs, rituals and practices belong to the food-gathering stage of human development, or with Hermes Trismegistus' supernatural world of magic and superstition. Alternatively, we may go back to the roots of our intolerance, the pious self-righteousness and bigotry of the Dark Ages' world-conquering religious fundamentalism; or equally well, we may start with the days steam power replaced the power of muscle, the bulk of Europe's population discovered the meaning of destitution, and Adam Smith proclaimed that the only legitimate function of government was 'the defence of the rich against the poor'.

Flying with Dylan Thomas, to a better world 'east of the sun, west of the moon, where each tomorrow dawns', may, on the other hand, take us beyond the third western age, the capitalist, beyond the second one, the Christian, and straight back to the first one, the ancient world of the Greeks. Each of the three epochs, Ernst Bloch, the German utopian Marxist held, valued different things: capitalism the capability to earn, the Middle Ages the capability to believe, and the Greeks the capability to enjoy.

Going back to the dawn of Western civilisation, the beginning, as Martin Heidegger, a major twentieth century philosopher held, of our 'spiritual-historical being' is going back to what 'predefined all subsequent ways of being and delineated our existence'. Greece is not the past, temples to be photographed by tourists in floral shirts and a Fuji Finepix in hand. Her exclusions, boundaries and demarcations, which have cast their spell over the millennia, continue to do so despite the globalisation tide; and if the future is not to be determined by madness, Greece is the power that still points to a world controlled by humans rather than theocracies, markets, systems or digital components.

Re-acquainting ourselves with the childhood of our civilisation can enable us to see everything once again in its aboriginal beauty with the fresh, vestal eyes of a child. The spirit of the founders of the Western world, the aspirations of its pioneers when individuation crossed the threshold into its actualisation, and Logos, the conscious self, came into being, can remind us of the road we all intended to travel before we lost our sense of direction. It can help us look for principles, 'reinvent' modernity and reconstruct society and culture. Despite history's radical discontinuity, the integrated recapture of the past, Adorno, Horkheimer and Marcuse argued, can well lead to a new harmonisation of our rational faculties and our sensuous nature. It can, so to speak, liberate sound from noise.

Greece, anything but perfect by our standards, has little to offer us in various areas. As it is, nothing comes in black and white as nothing that involves human relations can reach perfection. At best, it can approximate it. The dazzling rise of Greece to heights never reached before or since, is, however, too stunning to be affected by her own imperfections or others' misrepresentations of her; and her past, which is our own unfinished business, can still guide our future. It is a past which has the power to provide the theoretical framework for the creation of a genuinely different ethical reality, the model, as Michel Foucault held, of 'politics as ethics'. Foucault, incidentally, when asked in California, where he contracted HIV, if the Greeks offer an attractive and plausible alternative to our own culture, answered that he was not accepting the word 'alternative' because he was not in the 'history of solutions'.

Fluid and cheerful, the culture of Greece had nothing of the rigidity, the punctiliousness or the self-righteousness of the later ages. Rather than form, it rested on substance; rather than structures, on the spirit of man; and rather than textbooks and microprocessors, on human beings. From this point of view, rather than just a subject of study, Greece is also an ideal, 'just like the Holy Virgin', novelist Pavlos Matesis said frolicsomely, particularly 'as nobody ever saw her.'

The almost mythical journey of the Greeks into the future which turned them into Godlike figures begun with their liberation from religion. 'The weird and monstrous symbolism and imagery of the Gods and God monsters, and all the taboos and awes and restraints that had hitherto encumbered thinking', H.G. Wells, the science fiction writer and an outspoken socialist wrote, 'were here completely set aside.' The Gods were, of course, there but not as the creators of the world. The world had come before them and had, instead, created them the same way it had created the humans. The mortal Greeks owed nothing to the immortals. The force was *Anánke*, Necessity, which only needed to be understood and respected – not revered. This understanding gave the Greeks the freedom to search fearlessly for the truth and introduced Reason in the thinking of humanity. But Reason for the Greeks was Logos, an understanding rather than a philosophy, underpinned by respect for the workings of the universe that even the Gods could not disturb.

The philosophical abstraction behind their ethical understandings rested on the belief that everything was interconnected within the whole, which for the Greeks was a living organism. This whole embraced everything, nature and culture, soul and intellect, spirit and body, self and community, ends and means. Self-blossoming and abiding, diverse and perpetually evolving, it ensured that everything in it has its place, cherished for its intrinsic value rather than its benefits. Rather than its master, man was an integral part of this whole, and rather than in conflict, he had to live a life in tune with it to ensure that the balance of the natural order was not disturbed. Nature had in any case ensured that nothing in her domain would be disturbed whatever the intentions of its constituent parts. The elements of the whole kept within their own boundaries and respected the rights of the others, behaved, so to speak, in an ethical way. This was what man ought to do too.

Offences against the whole could not, therefore, be tolerated. They were hybris, and hybris was bound to be punished in what Solon, the Athenian statesman, called 'the court of time'. In the same way that winter could not appropriate the time allocated to spring, a citizen could not grab what belonged to his fellow-citizens and the desires of the flesh could not be allowed to control the whole person. Excess whether in the consumption of alcohol, the preoccupation with one's own looks or the use of power could not and would not be tolerated by the whole. Likewise, a dictatorship could never be sanctioned as a system to run a city. Citizens had natural rights, what today we call human rights; and democracy was the political embodiment of the natural order with Justice at its very heart. Justice, the child of necessity and a force superior to the will of both humans and the Gods, could not be accommodated in the house of profit.

Simple and frugal up to the end of the classical era, the life of the Greeks was guided by the principles of balance, proportion and symmetry leading to perfection: human perfection in all its forms, intellectual, moral, aesthetic, emotional and physical. This was the concept of *areté* lost completely in an age, ours, which seeks and finds fulfilment in shopping for things such as leather deck-shoes that yachtsmen wear even if the yacht that goes with them is unavailable.

Morality was an entirely human affair as the essentially secular culture of the Greeks ensured that no unaccountable power, divine or otherwise, could tell them what to think or how to behave. Though ever-present, the Gods had no power to demand adherence to a moral code written in stone or the wind. They lacked the kind of moral authority which contemporary religions have invested in their Gods. Humans were masters of their own fate, free to live their lives guided only by their own sense of right and good as determined by Reason. Reason had not just allowed the Greeks to embark upon their almost mythical journey into the mysteries of science, it also determined their morality. As Socrates held, acting on the strength of a true and rational judgment, man had to be good for his own good, his own happiness and welfare. Only the stupid would act otherwise, a person with low levels of MAOA, an enzyme essential for the proper working of the brain, as a contemporary neuroscientist would say.

At one with morality, Reason was the Greek 'God' without the Judaeo-Christian Godness, the 'God', in other words, which the triumph of the later 'true' religions forced into hiding. This understanding formed the foundations of their secular moral structure, which, underpinned by Justice, was endowed, like Byron's Constance Spencer Smith, with all the advantages of beauty, breeding and culture. The Greeks, incidentally, did not, and still do not, have in their vocabulary the word 'morality'. The only word is 'ethics', and their ethics had nothing to do with the knickers' morality of the Christians. Morality for them simply meant Justice. Hence no distinction was made between public morals and private pursuits.

The ethical ideal was embedded in the deeds of the individual embodying the unswerving commitment to both one's own higher self and the community. Happiness, personal autonomy, creativity, excellence, existence itself were inconceivable in any other context apart from that found within the community, the polis to which the citizens were attached as the tree is to its roots. The polis, the offspring of their perceptions and the mother of their achievements, the historic site which was the foundation and guardian of their superb civilisation, summed up the greatness of the human spirit and its potential. Athenian democracy, in particular, involved literally each and every citizen in its public affairs, from trade policy to diplomatic relations, from military campaigns to law court decisions, from artistic projects to civic duties and legislative matters. The citizen had direct access to power, shared its responsibility, was an integral and decisive part of the whole decision-making process. Fully involved, a master rather than a subject, he was, as a result, inspired, motivated, proud to belong, eager to contribute and willing to suffer. The polis was his polis. His were its successes as were its failures.

Athens, Herodotus wrote expressing 'thoughts that breathe' in 'words that burn', 'went from strength to strength, and proved, if proof were needed, how noble a thing freedom is, not in one respect, but in all.' As such, Greek democracy, Josiah Ober, professor of history at Princeton University, stated in the 1990s, provides the departure point for all those who refuse to accept the ever-expanding, hierarchical power of governments and corporations as an inevitable and natural outgrowth of social complexity. Its anti-bureaucratic, anti-secretive and anti-hierarchical nature, which all modern democracy refuses to be, is an eternal source of inspiration. So is its commitment to civic virtue.

The latter demanded just and honourable action irrespective

of achievements in the pursuit of the right and the good. A man had simply to do what a man had to do. Sincerity, truth, honesty, fairness, authenticity, loyalty, courage, Justice or any other quality presumed 'good' were not means in search of ends: they were ends in themselves, citizens of the Republic of Honour, inherently capable of giving life the meaning one looks in vain to find in the TV home of Big Brother, this contemporary temple of spiritual fulfilment.

The Greek culture, a culture of honour with an enduring appeal, placed the emphasis on character rather than personality, substance rather than image, doing rather than having, creating rather than consuming and becoming rather than being – 'become who you are' said Pindar, meaning that the potential is within us in seed form the moment we are born. As such it provided the inspiration, the 'ideal of that which we ourselves should like to produce', as Wilhelm von Humboldt, one of Germany's early liberal intellectual towers, put it a long time ago. It ensured the moral excellence of the individual.

The same culture valued simplicity, despised excess, treasured individuality within a community of human beings as opposed to human cyborgs, and looked forward to the satisfaction of all their needs. Rather than enrichment, consumption, showbiz, flat screen TV sets, miniature MP3 players or top-class lingerie, the ideal was self-realisation, the development of the individual's potentials to the full, and immortality through one's *oeuvre* in life. The immortality conferred upon the individual by an 'everflowing fame' was, according to Heraclitus, the thing chosen by the 'best'. Men of character could never let pleasure interfere with the pursuit of higher goals as much as they should never let work turn them into slaves. Retirement, as conventionally understood, University of Southern California professor James O'Toole said, was for the Greeks as much as it should be for us not an option. Retirement spent on the golf course is not a life well lived: teach, write, volunteer, learn, he suggested. Or, as Plato put it, 'a man who needs no longer to work for his living should practise excellence.'

The Greeks, Michel Foucault, the French lover of all refinements said, discovered 'the art of existence' – all those intentional and voluntary actions by which men not only set themselves rules of conduct, but also seek to transform themselves, to change themselves in their singular being, and to make their life into an *oeuvre* that carries certain aesthetic values and meets certain stylistic criteria. You just open the door to them and you let the spring come in.

Excellence, in this sense, was pursued for its pleasure rather than its benefits; and things were enjoyed for what they were, in their own right, rather than for the purpose they served. This aesthetic approach in response to the humans' needs, leading as Herbert Marcuse held, to the emancipation of the senses and the release of instinctual needs, was a prerequisite to the liberation of human nature, in itself a force of subversion of our corrupted culture. It was also the road leading to happiness, which as Aristotle held, is associated only with what we choose for itself, the thing itself being the leading of a just and honourable life, the growth of human potential, the passion for excellence which run in the Greek blood like an irresistible flood. Fulfilment in life meant transcending the self and fulfilling a meaning which was out there in the world rather than in one's own privacy. Happiness, personal satisfaction and fulfilment made sense only in the context of the community within which personal friendships were forged and only in the here and now. Children of immortality though they were, eternity was not the business of the Greeks.

The Greek journey had no need for a final destination – the purpose of the journey was the journey itself. Hence the Greeks never envisaged an idyllic future. Utopia did not exist for them. The Elysian fields at the far ends of the earth, a survivor of Minoan mythology, were as real to them in the classical era as Snow White and the seven dwarfs are to us. Even the word Utopia, though etymologically Greek in origin, was not part of their vocabulary – the word was invented by Thomas More in 1516. Excluding Plato, who in his *Politeia* produced a nightmare scenario which still haunts us, the Greeks did not need to dream of a better world; and certainly they did not need a life after life to compensate for a life lacking in the here-and-now.

Rather than a dogma in the form of an abstract, fixed and final objective, Utopia was for them a process in 'the fleeting moment of creation, which never stops' to borrow a Bergsonian expression. It was sought on earth rather than in heaven, in the here-and-now where all possibilities could be explored and all battles for their realisation entered into, in the present rather than the future, in their actions. They thus steered the boat as they sailed and ensured that change towards a just and honourable world took place every day. It is there when 'we' respect the rights of 'them', whether 'them' is women, consumers, ethnic minorities or foreign cultures, when the rights of the Third World to get affordable medicines are not annulled by something the West calls protection of intellectual property, or when our seasides are respected rather than violated by the furious forces of development. It is there, too, if and when we can appreciate rest as a time for silence and contemplation rather than as a means for recuperation for more work on the production line.

This is what Martin Heidegger had in mind when he said that the Greeks had achieved the 'unconcealedness of being', *aletheia*, the truth. Hence, his invitation to us to move like archaeologists into the Greek world, and leaping 'over the entire process of deformation and decay ... seek to reconquer the undestroyed power of naming in the language and its words'. The life of the Greeks, Hannah Arendt, the German-born political philosopher, also pointed out, confirmed the human condition – life itself, natality and mortality, worldliness, plurality and the earth, the individual's destiny independent from his creations, in the beauty of things neither necessary nor merely useful. These 'things' are, however, hiding in the immensity and intensity of the whole within which we have to address our enquiries.

Carried by the three horses of Oneness, Reason and Justice, the Greeks were able to ride into the spring meadows of their realities and myths, reach towards the outermost limit of daring across boundless expanses, and discover the truth of things never before seen. Their inspirational and colourful journey, their great wandering through life, filled them with optimism, their cohesion gave them a sense of direction, and the fertility of their intelligence engendered all the power they needed to handle successfully their relation with their Gods, the city-state and their inner selves. Hence their art expressed only harmony and beauty – inner horror, as pictured in the paintings of Edvard Munch's *The Scream* or Henry Fuseli's *The Nightmare*, were destined to be the products of a later age, ours.

Christianity, embodying, as Nietzsche said, 'the great revolt against noble values', transferred, however, life from the domain of the Earth to that of Heaven – its victory over the Greeks, he held, is in the historical roots of the present malaise. Wondering why the Germans could not be like the Greeks, German idealist philosopher Georg Wilhelm Hegel, too, blamed Christianity's transcendental values which, he said, split the individual from his community. Christianity dismissed Reason in favour of 'pure soul'. Morality was associated with the denial of life, and beauty was banned. Capitalism, and also socialism, subsequently restored Reason to its proper place, but in the process they desacrilised it, divorced it completely from any sense of morality and ends. The resulting crisis was not, however, a crisis of rationality, but a crisis of the mad 'rational' model created by modernity in its search for the unattainable.

The whole, which the Greeks associated with life itself, is, thus, no longer. Their impregnable belief in the intrinsic value of all things in life is extirpated, and the flag of Reason has turned grey. All that matters in its realm is mastery of the world associated with the clout of depravity, Bangkok by night, as the added bonus. Modernist Reason, an odious absurdity, has turned into something as clean as kosher pork.

Going back to the time when the dawn opened its petals and the day came to consciousness, to the unfenced existence of the early times which deny our tawdry and vulgar culture, is not a withdrawal into the realm of romantic fantasy. It is, instead, a move to the front line of the conflict against conglomerates, bureaucracies and experts, the ethos of the free market and the culture of apathy, disengagement and greed. It is what will enable us, American sociology professor George E. McCarthy said, 'to look more deeply into ourselves and our society, into contemporary institutions and crises, psychological repression and linguistic distortions, and political legitimation and capital accumulation.' The move may provide the inspiration needed to make another effort towards the revitalisation of civil society through what Montesquieu called 'the human passions which set it in motion', and it will certainly give us some solid ethical standards and even a shared sense of purpose. Standards accommodate a moral vocabulary which can give shape to new concepts.

We are all moderns now, says author Frederic Raphael; yet 'ancient ideas remain tenaciously relevant to modern life'. Hence the journey to the Greek past is a journey to the future which can give us back the sanity we have expelled from our lives, re-radicalise our thinking and help us to look forward with the fearless philosophical earnestness of the early years. This means getting in touch with the original intention and tuning in to the creative myth behind the miracle of the ages that even now, a time of transformation as profound as that which resulted from the Industrial Revolution, is still part of our inner selves. The Greek beginning, Heidegger said, does not lie behind us. It stands 'before us ... has passed in advance beyond all that is to come ... invaded our future. There it awaits us, as a distant command bidding us to catch up with its greatness'. If its power, he held, can never sustain itself, 'our decline ... is inevitable. But if its promise is to be brought to realisation, its insights, flowing from those initial wellsprings of understanding, need to be retrieved and restored.'

For some postmodernist writers, those who have nothing to say but still want to share it with the world, Heidegger's spirit, 'primordially Greek' and in search of an 'inner affinity' between Germany and Greece, exploited the 'opposition between Jerusalem and Athens' in the interests of anti-Semitism. The opposition they refer to is, indeed, there. It is, however, the opposition between a world dominated by the beneficiaries of Abraham's legacy, the dark, militant forces of religious revivalism, and a world committed to human values, the world of Prometheus, the hero of the Greeks, who, in the name of humanity, told the 'upstart Gods' to go to hell. It is in the struggle between these two forces that the immortal spirit of Greece may well come to our rescue and stop us slipping into a new dark age. Those who had nothing, not even a McDonald's half way through their ascent to eternity, may well, as George Seferis, the Greek poet would certainly say again, 'school us in serenity'.

Indeed, grasping the arm extended to us by our great philosophical and ethical tradition may well help us to re-establish the first principles and launch, as poet Friedrich Hölderlin, a partisan of the French revolution, had hoped, 'the forthcoming Revolution of attitudes and conceptions which will make everything that has gone before turn red with shame' In touch with immensity, 'unlessened', as he said, by time, the spirit of Greece, millennia before it was legally old enough to be the guardian of the human spirit, can transform and regenerate our culture, protect it against 'civilisation'. Greece's influence can be seen in Marx, too, whose 'guiding model', Hannah Arendt who shared his views on the subject, said, was 'doubtless the Athens of Pericles', except that in the communist society 'the privileges of the free citizens were to be extended to all'. Fundamentally Greek in its inspiration was, likewise, the 'Third Way' guru Alasdair MacIntyre's theory of ethics, or the latest in political theory – the 'deliberative democracy' introduced by Californian James Fishkin and tested in an Athens suburb in June 2006.

'Impelled by the crisis of our time, the crisis of the West', Leo Strauss, the German-Jewish historian of political philosophy, did also turn 'with passionate interest' towards the classical antiquity. Miserably, his own 'passionate interest' in it served only too well US President George W. Bush's effort to liberate Iraq from the Iraqis.

Greece, in a seductive diaphanous veil hiding the innocent beauty of her immortal spirit and in her brilliant apprehension of the present, keeps whispering to us, to use a George Seferis metaphor, 'like the breathing of the cypress tree that night, like the voice of the nocturnal sea on the pebbles, like the memory of your voice saying "happiness"'. Her whispers can be heard by the part of us which lives outside current times. Perhaps in response to them, Federico García Lorca, the celebrated Spanish poet and dramatist, decided to 'go very far, farther than those hills, farther than the seas, close to the stars, to beg Christ the Lord to give back the soul I had of old, when I was a child'. Greece, the child, was in her innocence more mature than the old world of our time.

The divinity of Greece is, of course, beyond our current experience and comprehension. Though the meaning and purpose her culture generated is, like the air in our lungs, always there, the escape from the cage of our artificial existence to the roots of our culture, into a past which for many embodies the best the human race has ever achieved, is not easy. Even the hopelessly easy promiscuity of our time's sympathies cannot be of any great help. As French novelist André Gide said, to begin with nothing is harder than to get outside one's epoch in order to perceive the shortcomings common to a whole generation. We are all prisoners of time or just too busy with things like asset-backed securitisation, management buyouts, and structuring and marketing OTC derivatives to think of something else. Greece, 'the lightning that mocks the night' as Shelley would have it is, indeed, beyond the range of our reality's long fingers, 'beyond the Western stars', as Euripides would have said. The contemporary world has no centre, which for the Greeks was their mythology. It is too heterogeneous, and also too polarised, to ensure adherence to the same set of principles; and society today, so fragmented, is not a unity nurturing a natural harmony of interests.

Equally true, Greece has been placed beyond us not just by time, innocent of any misdemeanour, but also by the meagreness, the reduced circumstances of the present. Sadly, as Byron bemoaned, with things as they are 'nor can we be what we recall, nor dare we think on what we are'. Being a Greek myself does not place me ahead of anybody else in the effort to cut and extirpate mountains of forgetfulness. Indeed, reaching 'as far back as the memory of freedom', filling a vacuum drained of the past was probably more difficult for me than it was for Milton, Erasmus, Hölderlin or Goethe, Byron, Shelley or Marx, Hegel, Nietzsche, Proust, Heidegger, Marcuse or Ezra Pound.

At school I was taught the classics, a 'departed worth' seemingly of no relevance to anything, but just like all the other kids, blinded by poverty or a banausic Marxism which I grew to hate as much as my shortcomings, I just did not want to embarrass myself by taking an interest in them. The radiant breath of the ancient monuments under which we played as children and dated as teenagers, the sites where Cleisthenis had thundered, Aristotle had proposed to Mrs Aristotle or the young Athenians staged their torch races in the evening on horseback, were as remote from us as we are from our homeless future. 'The way we, words, ideas have declined', poet Yannis Ritsos melancholically reflected, 'we can't be bothered with old or recent glories.' In spite of the linguistic continuity thriving across the millennia, for the modern Greeks to relate either psychologically, spiritually or intellectually to the ancient world is an impossibility. Memories have been disloyal or rather we have been disloyal to them. The scent of mint lingering around their aura has dissipated.

Nevertheless, and most embarrassingly for me, I did discover the pristine freshness of ancient Greece, her prismatic light and gratifying world, but only after my arrival in England. It was then, and only then, that I reconnected with an imperishable world chiselled upon the rocks of time. Greece's mountains, small when I had left the country, reached for the heights deserved for our winged prayers. But it was then that I also discovered the perennial value of the world of the Greeks, the amarant 'glory', to borrow a line from Edgar Alan Poe, 'that was Greece', the tale that can shape our future. It is this tale, which, as Brecht would have said, cannot be weighed like pills with a precision scale, which can provide us with the inspiration for a new beginning.

The ideal, Odysseus' Ithaca, the final destination, may of course never be reached. But even if it is not, it is not Ithaca that matters. It is, instead, the journey to it, i.e. the journey to our essence, or at least the part of us which modernity has not contaminated. It is what may help us at least to disengage from false pretences, so akin to stupidity as novelist Marcel Proust has attested. Ithaca, if you reach it, may be poor, Kavafis says in one of his most celebrated poems, but Ithaca has not deceived you. The wages of your labour are the journey itself, a treasure of delight and a mine of entertainment, the joy of entering harbours you've never seen before, the sensational discoveries, the omnifarious experiences, the conquest of wisdom. Although his intrepidity did not agree with Kavafis' mellifluousness, Nietzsche's approach was not all that different. 'The secret of realising the greatest fruitfulness and enjoyment of existence', he said, 'is to live dangerously. Build', he urged his readers in his masterful lyrical style, 'your cities on the slopes of Vesuvius! Send your ships into uncharted seas! Live in conflict with your equals and yourself!' Do also, perhaps, collect all the facts, the dead wood of pragmatism stored in the soul, and one cold night burn them to see light.

The journey, as hazardous as Odysseus', requires the courage of a few genuine convictions, evident, I hope, in this book. Written not from an 'objective', languorous, detached point of view and free from lesser calculations, it is being sent to battle on the crimson frontiers of the unattainable. Like Nietzsche, who 'did not know what purely intellectual problems are', I have written it, also like him, with 'my whole heart and soul'. Life is too rich, intense and vibrant to watch as a disinterested observer; too thriving to sustain with halfwitted trivialities; and too capacious to abandon for spiritual indigence. Although it took me time to discover it, for a single, heterosexual male, it is also too good to abandon in order to write about it.

Yet, armed fundamentally with the power, or rather the mescalin intensity of my illusions, this is exactly what I did during a night that lasted a few years. In this book and the other two that follow, all of them my 'little cargo of hopes and fears', I try to articulate the thesis I have already advanced in the preceding chapters. The attempt may sound like Adam's recollection of his fall. But it is fuelled by hope.

Antonio Gramsci's 'pessimism of the intellect' is, indeed, accompanied by the 'optimism of the will' to which I remain as committed as to my very best sins.

Index

In Bed With Madness: Trying to make sense in a world that doesn't *by Yannis Androcopoulos*

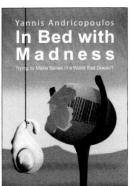

Globalism endowed us with McDonald's, 'the world's local bank', English football teams without English players and an irrepressible desire for more as enough is never good enough – the blanket is always too short. Our personal world as much as our social and political realities seem to have blithely surrendered to the madness of a civilization which views anything from corporate greed and global warming to military adventures and religious fundamentalism as normal as a door banging in the wind. The destructive capabilities of our age have run too far ahead of our wisdom. However, the process is not irreversible if our thinking can postpone its retirement. *In Bed with Madness* is 'a well-argued, powerful and profound indictment of contemporary culture', stylishly written – a reviewer said he would have bought it just for its humour!

200 pp., £8.95 / $17.90, 978-1845401290 (pbk.)

The Greek Inheritance: Ancient Greek wisdom for the digital era *by Yannis Androcopoulos*

The culture of ancient Greece, a culture of joy, was replaced by the Judaeo-Christian culture of faith and then by the capitalist culture of profit. Yet it is the only culture worth fighting for if we want a world run by humans rather than theocracies, nanotechnologies or private equity funds. Yannis Andricopoulos views the Greek culture as the front line of the battle against individualism, materialism, authoritarianism and religious extremism. In a world turned into the corporations' playground, this is also the battle for human values, civic virtues and an ethical society. *The Greek Inheritance* traces the conflict between Greek values and those of the repressive, religious or capitalist order throughout the millennia. The book is challenging and well-written with a light, humorous touch.

260 pp., £8.95 / $17.90, 978-1845401306 (pbk.)

The Future of the Past: From the culture of profit to the culture of joy *by Yannis Androcopoulos*

Universalism in its old forms has, just like door-to-door milkmen, gone for good. But the search for some universally accepted ethical standards cannot be abandoned – values are not colourless as the wind and odourless as thoughts. Looking into our world from the classical Greek point of view, Yannis Andricopoulos wonders whether we cannot place Justice again at the heart of our morality, look forward to the happiness of the individual rather than the upgrading of his or her consumer fantasies, and endeavour to create, not more wealth, but a just and honourable world. *The Future of the Past* is written in 'a lively, challenging style guaranteeing to stimulate debate on the most pressing issues of our time'.

Yannis Androcopoulos Ph.D, co-founder of Skyros holidays, is a former political journalist and editor of i-to-i magazine.

200 pp., £8.95 / $17.90, 978-1845401313 (pbk.)

Imprint Academic, PO Box 200, Exeter, EX5 5HE, UK   Tel: +44 (0)1392 851550
imprint-academic.com/skyros

Yannis Andricopoulos was born in Athens where he spent the formative years of his life – years scarred by wars, deprivation and political repression. 'We managed to survive', he says, 'but only on grains of hope.'

In 1964 he entered journalism with *Avghi*, an Athens daily, and in 1967 arrived in swinging London as his newspaper's correspondent. The happy event was, however, shortlived, for the Greek military dictatorship (1967-1974) deprived him of his nationality. His actions, the colonels claimed, 'were detrimental to the interests of Greece'. Forced to stay in the UK as a political refugee, he completed a Ph.D. in Diplomatic History at Birkbeck College, University of London, and also headed the Greek National Union of Students in exile (1969-1971). The latter's activities caused his expulsion from three East European countries.

In 1974, when the military regime collapsed, he resumed his career as London-based foreign correspondent first for *Avghi* and later for *Eleftherotypia*, another Athens daily. In the same year he published his first book in Athens, an edited version of prime minister Churchill's personal papers on 1944 Greece. As a historian he has since published another three books on 20th century Greek and European history and as a journalist he has reported from various troublespots in the world. On meeting prime minister Margaret Thatcher at 10 Downing Street, unable all of a sudden to work out whether she was a prime minister or a prime ministress, he could not open his mouth. Thankfully, she saved him with her kindness.

In 1979 he co-founded *Skyros*, the holistic community-based holiday centre on the Greek island of Skyros, which he still co-directs, and ten years later, from 1989 to 1994, was also the editor of *i-to-i* magazine, an alternative London publication. He is still a Greek citizen because, he says, he wants to cheer for Greece without feeling guilty when Greece plays against England. He now lives in the Isle of Wight where he co-founded *The Grange*, a small seaside centre offering various personal development courses.

The three books of this series have been inspired by both his involvement in the truculent world of politics and the graceful, personal world of Skyros.